THIS WORLDWIDE CONSPIRACY

by

IVOR BENSON

Copyright (C) Ivor Benson 1972

This worldwide conspiracy for the overthrow of civilisation and for the reconstitution of society on the basis of arrested development, of envious malevolence and impossible equality.—Winston Churchill.

Printed and Published by
NEW TIMES LIMITED
P.O. Box 1226L, Melbourne, Victoria 3001

In Association with
DOLPHIN PRESS (PTY.) LTD.,
P.O. Box 3145, Durban, South Africa.

ISBN: 978-2-925611-05-9
Printed in the USA.

THE AUTHOR

Ivor Benson is a well-known South African journalist with several years of Fleet Street experience. A former Chief Assistant Editor of The Rand Daily Mail, Johannesburg, he came into great prominence in 1964 when he delivered news commentaries from Radio South Africa and was afterwards employed by the Rhodesian Government as Information Adviser.

Mr. Benson has travelled extensively in Africa and has witnessed at close quarters some of the major development of recent years, including the Congo turmoil of 1960.

THE BOOK

Much of the material in this little book has already been published, in one form or another, in *Behind the News,* a monthly newsletter produced by Ivor Benson and airmailed as a personal service to a widening circle of subscribers all over the world.

The book will, therefore, serve as an introduction to the newsletter which provides a running commentary on important news of the day, filling in some of the missing facts and combining all in a picture of the contemporary scene which makes sense.

THE AUTHOR

Ivor Benson is a well-known South African journalist with several years of Fleet Street experience. A former Chief Assistant Editor of The Rand Daily Mail, Johannesburg, he came into great prominence in 1963 when he delivered news commentaries from Radio South Africa and was afterwards employed by the Rhodesian Government as Information Adviser.

Mr. Benson has travelled extensively in Africa and has witnessed at close quarters some of the major development of recent years, including the Congo turmoil of 1960.

Behind the News is a monthly newsletter airmailed to subscribers as a personal service.

Subscription Rates: South Africa R2.25. Rhodesia $2.25. U.K. R.260. Europe R2.72. Australia & New Zealand R3.20. U.S.A. & Canada $5.00.

Obtainable from *Dolphin Press (Pty.) Ltd.,* P.O. Box 3145, Durban, South Africa.

For nothing is secret, that shall not be made manifest; neither anything hid, that shall not be known and come abroad.— Luke 8.17.

Contents:

SOME DARE CALL IT CONSPIRACY

> *So you see . . . that the world is governed by very different personages to what is imagined by those who are not themselves behind the scenes.—Benjamin Disraeli, former Prime Minister of England.*

THERE are only two ways of trying to explain contemporary history.

One is that history is the product of blind chance, or of forces entirely outside our control.

This has been called "the idiot theory of history" and is promoted most zealously by the mass media of the Liberal Establishment all over the world.

The other view is that while it is true accident or chance always have some contribution to make to the end result, much of what has been happening in the world, and continues to happen, can only be explained as the product of ingenious long-range planning.

Leftists who continue to attack what they like to describe as "the much-discredited conspiracy theory" need to catch up with their own leftist reading.

What they don't seem to know is that one of the greatest living spokesmen of the left, Dr. Carroll Quigley, Professor of History at the Foreign Service School at Georgetown University, U.S.A., and a highly placed Liberal Establishment "insider", has bluntly admitted the truth of what conservatives have been saying for years.

In his massive book "Tragedy and Hope — a History of the World in our Time", Dr. Quigley writes:

> "I know of the operations of this network because I have studied it for 20 years and was permitted for two years, in the early 1960's to examine its papers and secret records. I have no aversion to it or to most of its aims and have, for much of my life, been close to it and to many of its instruments. I have objected both in the past and recently to a few of its policies . . .

but in general my chief difference of opinion is that it wishes to remain unknown, and I believe its role in history is significant enough to be known" (P 953).

Dr. Quigley speaks with authority when he admits that the super-capitalists of this "network" have worked in close partnership with Communists and Socialists in the United States, explaining, however, that "the power these energetic leftists exercised was never their own power or Communist power but was ultimately the power of the international financial coterie".

This, too, leading conservatives have been saying for years — Communism is not a power in its own right, but is only an instrument, or part of a much bigger conspiracy.

Another Liberal Establishment "insider", Dr. Nicholas Murray Butler, President of Columbia University, nominated for that post by J. P. Morgan and Co. of Wall Street, has made this interesting pronouncement: "The world is divided into three kinds of people — a very small group that *makes* things happen, a somewhat larger group that *watches* things happen, and a great multitude that never knows what has happened".

It is the purpose of this little book to increase the number of those who watch things happen and understand what they see.

These, after all, are the only ones who can hope to be able to influence the way things happen.

And it goes without saying that the few who *make* things happen would much rather not be watched at all.

Surely, then, we have only ourselves to blame if, knowing all this, we finish up confused, sick at heart and powerless, with that great multitude that never knows what has happened.

THE BATTLEGROUND OF THE MIND

That we have attained the final step on the evolutionary ladder of war is most unlikely. For mechanical and chemical weapons may disappear and be replaced by others more terrible. This method of imposing the will of one man on another may in turn be replaced by purely psychological warfare wherein weapons are not even used or battlefields sought or loss of life and limb aimed at. But in its place the corruption of human reason, the dimming of the human intellect and the disintegration of the moral and spiritual life of one nation by the will of another is accomplished.

—General J. F. C. Fuller, in his book *Tanks in the Great War.*

TARGET No. 1 for modern revolutionary forces is the mind and soul of man.

People must be persuaded to permit and even help promote those changes in society required by the conspirators.

No one understood this better than Winston Churchill, who in 1920 as Secretary for War and Air in the British Government, had unequalled access to top-secret military, police and diplomatic intelligence on the Bolshevik Revolution in Russia.

Writing in the *Illustrated Sunday Herald* of February 8, 1920, Churchill threw a great deal of light on what he described as "this worldwide conspiracy for the overthrow of civilisation and for the reconstitution of society on the basis of arrested development, of envious malevolence and impossible equality . . ."

All this is being achieved today in a variety of ways.

The first and most obvious way to influence the individual is through his mind, that is, his ordinary thinking and opinion-forming processes.

If he can be persuaded by the newspapers he reads or
by other media of mass communication to permit and even
help to promote changes in society which are harmful to
himself and to his community, then he can be said to be
already in a state of "arrested development".

For it is surely obvious that the fully developed
individual knows what is best for himself and his community
and therefore cannot be manipulated like a puppet by those
who have succeeded in placing themselves at all the main
avenues of access to his mind!

This kind of mind control, however, can only be of a
temporary nature; much more is needed if people are to be
led or pushed all the way into what Churchill called
"A reconstituted society", in other words, a world which
has undergone revolutionary changes.

What is needed is a form of psychological warfare which
undermines the individual at depth, reducing him to a state
of "arrested development" from which there is no quick and
easy escape.

Instead of being deceived, like the victim of any ordinary
confidence trickster, he is demoralised and thereby made
more vulnerable than ever to all the arts of persuasion and
deceit practised by the professional opinion makers.

Part of the story of how all this is done will be found
in the chapters of this book.

Instead of the cultural exercise and education he must
have if he is to unfold all the rich possibilities of his nature,
he is supplied almost exclusively with a spurious substitute,
a cunningly concocted anti-culture.

His literature is poisoned, and his art and his music;
and massive pressure and propaganda, including the promotion of habit-forming drugs, are used to sever all those
ties which join him to his family, his nation and his race,
thus reducing him to a more or less permanent condition
of "arrested development".

But who is behind all this revolutionary activity? The
following will provide part of the answer to that question.

TWO FACES OF REVOLUTION

Jerry Rubin, the bearded American revolutionary
whose book *"Do It!"*, inciting to urban guerilla warfare, is
now to be seen in Establishment book stores all over the

U.S.A., is a great admirer of American radio and television. He has described television as "a commercial for the revolution", explaining: "Every revolution needs a colour TV".

In his book, he praises Walter Cronkite of the Columbia Broadcasting System News as the best organiser for the revolutionary Students for a Democratic Society (SDS), and praises him for bringing out, from time to time, the map of the United States "with circles around the campuses which blew up today".

If the revolutionaries themselves personally owned the three great radio and television networks — CBS, NBS and ABC — these networks could not be used more effectively to undermine a generation and help create the sort of conditions which revolution requires.

Writes Gary Allen in *American Opinion:* "The media sell Marxists to the public as innocent and idealistic reformers even as they depict conservatives and anti-Communists as diabolical conspirators . . . It is no wonder that Vice-President Agnew's attack on the media was received with enthusiasm by so many Americans. He dared to tell the truth — that the country is being psychologically sabotaged from within. What seems to have caused the most frenzy among the media, however, is the fact that the Vice-President indicated the slanting of the news is conspiratorial in nature. He spoke of the 'tiny, enclosed fraternity of privileged men in New York and Washington whose power is absolute', and who decide what 40- to 50-million Americans will learn of the day's events in the nation and in the world".

The Establishment places the vast resources of modern radio and television at the service of those whose frankly declared aim it is to "destroy the Establishment".

The people of America are left with this question: Is it not possible that the Establishment and the Revolution are one and the same thing, or two different aspects of the same set of moneyed forces?

If there is any reliable answer to that question, it must be sought in an investigation of the ownership of the major radio and television networks in the United States and an exploration of the relationship of that ownership and the great concentrations of financial power which constitute the Establishment.

The most powerful of the three networks is the Columbia Broadcasting System (CBS), whose empire comprises TV outlets in New York, Los Angeles, Chicago, Philadelphia and St. Louis, and 200 affiliated stations all over the United States. The big boss of CBS is William S. Paley, son of Samuel and Gold Palinsky, who came to America from Russia before the turn of the century. Sam, who became a wealthy cigar manufacturer, bought the infant CBS from Paramount Pictures and later put his son William in charge. Among the big shareholders is the international banking firm of Lehman Brothers, a satellite of the world-wide Rothschild investment network. Another big shareholder is Dr. Leon Levy, William Paley's brother-in-law.

A whole book could be written about Paley's dubious background, but we have space here only for one significant paragraph which tells the whole story. Mr. Paley was identified with the Institute of Pacific Relations which a Senate Internal Security Sub-Committee described as follows: "The IPR has been considered by the American Communist Party and by Soviet officials as an instrument of Communist policy, propaganda and military intelligence. . . The IPR was a vehicle used by the Communists to orientate American Far Eastern policy towards Communist objectives".

The result, as we all know, was a Communist take-over in China.

The CBS is the world's biggest producer of gramophone records, and by its advertising of culturally subversive pop music is the main supporter of America's "underground press". CBS is also the world's largest exporter of films, especially those used for television. Also a financial backer of CBS is the Harriman banking empire; the older Harriman worked closely with Jacob Schiff of Kuhn, Loeb and Company, one of the main financiers of the Bolshevik Revolution.

The rest of the CBS story reads like a report of evidence before the Un-American Activities Committee.

No. 2 in order of importance is the National Broadcasting Corporation (NBC), which is a subsidiary of the giant Radio Corporation of America (RCA), a huge producer of films, gramophone records and other forms of package "entertainment", better described, perhaps, as "cultural subversion". The big boss of NBC is David Sarnoff, promoted in one jump from civvy street to the rank of

Brigadier-General in the American Army by Mr. F. D. Roosevelt during World War II.

Sarnoff's biography was written by Eugene Lyons, former editor of *Soviet Russia Pictorial* and a director of the Soviet *Tass* agency. Sarnoff, we learn, was born in Uzlian, Minsk, Russia, the son of Lena Pivin. Directors of RCA, the parent company, have included Andre Meyer of Lazard Freres, Stephen M. du Brul of Lehman Brothers, and Lewis L. Strauss, a partner of Kuhn, Loeb and Company.

For more than ten years the vice-president of NBC was Alfred R. Stern, son of Marion Rosenwald Stern, daughter of Julius Rosenwald of the Sears Roebuck fortune. *The National Encyclopaedia of American Biography* says that Alfred's grandfather, Julius Rosenwald, gave $6m. to Stalin for "re-colonisation within the Soviet Union"; other donors to the same cause were financiers Felix Warburg, Louis Marshall, Herbert Lehman and John D. Rockefeller.

"Like many of the financiers of the revolution in America today", writes Gary Allen, "Stern's grandfather set up a tax-free foundation to finance his pet Communist causes". His donations to Communism in America are reckoned in millions of dollars.

The new power in RCA is David Sarnoff's son Robert, married in 1950 to Felicia Schiff Warburg, daughter of Paul Felix Warburg of Kuhn, Loeb and Company; Felicia is the great-granddaughter of Trotsky's financial angel Jacob Schiff.

The last of the big three networks, much smaller than the other two, is American Broadcasting Corporation (ABC) which has 153 primary television affiliates, a chain of 399 cinemas, and is one of the world's biggest producers of gramophone records, likewise lavishly advertised in underground revolutionary papers through its ads promoting "acid rock music".

This will help to explain our own frequently repeated definition of Communism as "an imperialism of money of the highest order of magnitude and concentration of control, using as one of its instruments the revolutionary dregs of human society".

THE SOCIALIST TRAP

> *Tseu-Lou asked: If the Prince of Mei appointed you head of the government, what would be your first task?*
>
> *Kung Fu Tse replied: Make sure that things are called by their proper names, make sure that terminology is exact.*
>
> *—The Analects, ch.xv.*

IN the realm of mind or intellect, as distinct from soul or personality, there can be no doubt that one of the most potent weapons being used against the West is socialist ideology or idealism.

In its frankly revolutionary form, this ideology is known as Marxism-Leninism, or, simply as Communism.

In its evolutionary form, in which systematic penetration and undermining of existing institutions is preferred to hastier, more violent methods, it is better known as Fabian Socialism, or simply Socialism.

The tactics dictated by circumstances may be different, but the end result is the same — the socialist state, according to a declared Communist like Karl Marx or a Fabian like Professor Harold Laski. The real motives are the same and the forces behind the motives are the same.

The battle against those who use this socialist ideology as a weapon must therefore begin in the human mind. We can never win by merely raising defences against this weapon; we must learn how to disarm it, render it no longer effective as a weapon of psychological warfare.

Why is it that this socialist ideology works like a drug on millions of well-meaning, serious-minded people in the Western world?

This was a question put to the present writer by General Hendrik van den Bergh, South Africa's Chief of the Security Police, a few years ago, shortly after he and his men had swooped on a luxurious residence in semi-rural

Rivonia, near Johannesburg, delivering a smashing blow at the Communist underground.

"The police alone cannot win this battle", he said. "We must also win on the battleground of the mind. We must understand what it is that makes Communist propaganda so effective, especially among our young people in the universities".

Our reply to General Van den Bergh's question may need a lot of explaining, but it can be compressed into a few words: There is a colossal misunderstanding, involving the meaning of words.

Marxism-Leninism and other forms of international Communism exploit a fact of overpowering importance: Most people, and Western Europeans most of all, are "socialists" at heart, but they are "ethical socialists"; they are revolted by the unbridled competitiveness of modern industrial-commercial society, the principal motivation of which is personal wealth and personal power.

Especially when young and unspoiled, they experience an irrepressible yearning for a form of society in which the individual finds in the service of his community the maximum fulfilment of his own being.

Many of our young people cannot distinguish the ethical socialism for which they yearn and the leftist state-ownership socialism which they are offered. It is a smart fish which can distinguish a fine piece of food which it wants and needs from another, similar in taste and appearance, which conceals an angler's hook!

Behind the spurious idealism, behind the pie-in-the-sky —the actuality! The socialism of leftist propaganda is an economic totalitarianism in which the human individual is degraded to the status of a unit of labour. As experienced by the individual, it is simply a bureaucratic tyranny.

As there is one "socialism" which stands for the maximum liberation and fulfilment of human vitality and another which stands for the total enslavement of the individual, so there are also two "capitalisms"—or, rather, two things which are totally different but sharing one name.

There is private enterprise capitalism which is inseparable from genuine ethical socialism, and international finance capitalism which is inseparable from the Communist conspiracy.

There is, of course, far more to it than that. As we pointed out in another article, our young people need to be able to distinguish between a genuine political idealism and a spurious one.

Admittedly, this is not easy. The counterfeit coin or forged banknote is deliberately made to look as like the genuine article as possible. Some forged banknotes are so well made that only an expert can tell the difference.

It is the same with political "idealism". The spurious one is made to correspond as closely as possible with the genuine one, so much so that exceptional powers of penetration are called for if the difference is to be detected.

One of the secrets of the tremendous appeal of Fabian and Marxist socialism is that it appeals directly to something in the nature of Western man which could be called "socialist" — if that word itself had not been disvalued by base associations. Let us rather, then, call it a "Social Ethic". Some writers have gone so far as to call it "Ethical Socialism" to distinguish it from the socialism preached by the enemies of the West.

There can be no doubt that capitalism as being experienced all over the Western world today is thoroughly rotten — and it is the very forces which helped to make it rotten which, pretending to want to sweep it away with revolution, conspire to bring it to the end state of a totalitarian finance capitalism — which is what we find behind the Iron Curtain.

A genuine social ethic (for ethical socialism), while recognising that the individual finds his highest fulfilment in serving the group, also recognises that private ownership and private enterprise, implying an element of competition among individuals, are the keys which unlock energy and imagination.

In case some of our readers still find it hard to believe that socialism is the instrument rather than the enemy of international finance capitalism, we quote a paragraph from *Time* magazine:

> Four decades of Social Democrats have governed Sweden, but four generations of Wallenbergs have controlled much of it. In a country where socialism is as familiar as smorgasbord the 202-year-old dynasty retains a remarkable grip: complete or partial control of 30

major Swedish firms, including nine of the country's 15 largest. For all the Wallenberg's influence, the family bank, Stockholm's Enskilda is relatively small.

Reporting plans for the merger of the Wallenbergs' Stockholm Enskilda Bank with Sweden's second largest bank Skandinavska Banken, the magazine explains that the Wallenbergs are now likely to become more powerful than ever since the other partner in the new bank has interests in 28 major firms, one of the largest of these (which hitherto escaped Wallenberg control) being Volvo, the car manufacturers.

Why, it will be asked, do we recommend this report to the attention of modern youth? Our answer: Because it contains a message which modern educated youth needs. We refer in particular to all those who march behind leftist banners.

The target of their political animosity in all the Western countries, so they tell us, is "monopoly capitalism". And what is the alternative? What is it the left promotes with so much enthusiasm? They tell us themselves: it is socialism, even communism.

All our leftist intellectuals, young and old, continue to regard socialism in one form or another as the alternative to capitalism.

The story from Sweden, like hundreds of similar stories which could be told, brings to their attention — if only they will open their minds for a moment — the important message that there *is no real antagonism between socialism* and what they call capitalism.

What this means is that modern rebellious youth (and many older people, including ministers of religion and university professors) have been duped by the very forces against which they imagine they are rebelling.

By offering them socialism, even communism, as an alternative and remedy for a sick capitalism, even communism, the Establishment has largely succeeded in taking over the very rebellion of the mind and spirit which might have threatened their existence.

Sweden offers a glaring example of what has been happening in many parts of the world in the last half-century. In Sweden we see clearly what socialism really means — monopoly capitalism unequalled in any other country this side of the Iron Curtain and the reduction of 95% of the population to a highly sophisticated form of serfdom.

Is that what our rebellious youth want, when they call for the replacement of "monopoly capitalism" with "the ideal of socialism"?

Certainly not! They have something quite different in mind. By socialism they mean what the lying propagandists of the super-rich say but do not mean: A shared ownership of the means of production and distribution; *"from each according to his ability, to each according to his need"*.

There are signs today, however, that many young liberals are at last becoming disenchanted. When that happens they realise that it is the conservatives alone who have been fighting the real battle against those responsible for a *status quo* which is fast becoming unbearable.

Examples to parallel that of Sweden can be found from all parts of the world.

Only a couple of years ago the Zambian government decided to nationalise that country's rich copper industry, ownership and control of which were always shared by South Africa's Anglo American Corporation and Roan Selection Trust — two giants of monopoly capitalism if ever there were any.

Anglo American, like the Wallenbergs, has an almost total stranglehold on the economy of South Africa, including gold and diamond mining. RST is only a branch of the still bigger American Metal Climax, an industrial and financial empire with worldwide ramifications.

Did AA and RST raise loud cries of protest at the enforced expropriation in Zambia? Was there any objection from the mass media of the "capitalist" world when the Zambian government simply helped itself to 51% of the shares in the copper mining companies? We believe the companies suggested the deal. The shares did not even have to be paid for! As a Zambian government statement explained: "They will be paid for out of future profits".

Anglo American has continued ever since the "take-over" of the copper mines to expand its holdings in Zambia, nor will AA mind in the least if these, too, are socialised in turn.

And why doesn't Anglo-American mind? For the simple reason that Anglo American knows what socialism really means. Why should AA and RST mind the "take-over" of their copper mines by a puppet government in Zambia which they and their international financial associates themselves own and control?

The only difference is that the control in the hands of AA and RST is now more secure than ever.

This explains the leftist politics of Harry Oppenheimer, multi-millionaire head of the Anglo American Corporation.

Oppenheimer is all on the side of rebellious youth because he is confident that with his money he can control their rebellion and harness it to his own purposes. The wonder is that our young rebels can be so foolish that they could even applaud this pillar of monopoly capitalism when he spoke as he did in 1968 at the University of Natal:

> It must be intolerable to students that governments, irrespective of party, should accept "this sorry state of things entire" and should limit themselves to social tinkering, when they ought, as they see it, "to shatter it to bits and then remould it nearer to the heart's desire". Isn't it right that these opinions should be strongly felt? Isn't it right that they should be expressed forcefully and fearlessly?

A perfect example of international finance capitalism speaking the language of the leftist, revolutionary anti-capitalists!

IT'S 1984 IN SWEDEN NOW!

There is a whole world of difference between a socialist idealism "in glorious Technicolor" as promised by the propagandists and the socialist system as finally delivered.

This is something the Swedes have found out for themselves to their lasting grief. They do not have to wait for George Orwell's 1984 — they have it already, a bureaucratic tyranny ten times more heartless and oppressive than any one-man dictatorship.

The whole sad story is told by Roland Huntford, Stockholm correspondent of *The Observer* (London), a man who can hardly be accused of any rightwing bias, in his latest book *The New Totalitarians*.

Here are only a few points taken from a review of Huntford's book by Charles Curran, M.P., in the *Sunday Telegraph*:

● *The state strives as a matter of deliberate policy to break down individuality and liquidate the family.*

● It has set up a Directorate of Social Affairs, ruled and run by socialist intellectuals, which has untrammelled power over the custody of children. It can remove any child from his or her home by administrative order against which there can be no appeal to the courts or anywhere else. Parents go in constant fear of having their children taken away from them if their methods of upbringing do not conform absolutely to the required ideas — that is, socialist ideas.

● To breed docile citizens, Socialist Sweden uses the schools. Private schools are being eliminated. The State comprehensives are a matrix for manufacturing egalitarian uniformity — de-Christianised, amoral, where children learn that copulation is a therapeutic activity, like eating and taking exercise.

● To keep its adults docile, Sweden uses housing policy. It aims at a population of tenants in State flats, mixed together so as to destroy class differences. "People must give up the right to choose their neighbours", says the intellectual who heads the National Planning Directorate.

● "Sweden is a spiritual desert", says Huntford. It has a suicide rate of 22 per 100,000 (third highest in the world); it mass-produces drunkards; its crime rate rose 250% between 1950 and 1966; it is plagued with juvenile delinquents and a "catastrophic increase" in gonorrhoea among its emancipated schoolchildren.

Stephen Croall, Stockholm correspondent of the liberal *Guardian* says that a mental health investigation carried out by Dr. Hans Lohman, considered one of Sweden's top experts in psychiatry and socio-medicine, "paints a gloomy picture of a merciless, unfriendly society".

The latest figures show that the number of in-patients admitted to mental institutions rose from 73,000 in 1969 to 83,000 in 1970. A still greater number of out-patients were given "light psychiatric care", while the "enormous number" who took to alcohol or drugs as a "way out" are not included in the statistics.

Dr. Lohman describes "a hard and regulated society in which the citizens must maintain production and performance or be rejected as someone no longer useable".

In a word — a slave society administered on behalf of the faceless slave-masters of cosmopolitan international finance by a class of privileged slaves or janissaries, the so-called leftist intellectuals.

The Swedes, one of the most gifted and energetic people, have been made the victims precisely of that which hitherto down the ages has given them most strength — their homogeneity, or relative racial purity.

Like South Sea Islanders who had no inborn defences against Europe's childhood ailments, the Swedes with their long history of isolation had no inborn protection against cosmopolitan influences which have been spread worldwide by our technical-industrial-commercial civilisation.

It is no accident of history that Mediterranean countries like Spain, Portugal, and Greece, are among the nations best able to defend their cultural integrity.

In Sweden today we see what is produced in the end by money and a rootless intellect which it can so easily purchase and harness to its purposes.

We do not have to go to Sweden to find out, nor do we have to rely on writers from other countries, like Roland Huntford. The Swedish establishment's own newspapers themselves tell us, because the facts cannot be hidden. Nor is it necessary to read scores of newspapers when one article in one newspaper can sometimes give us a clear glimpse of the total reality.

Thus, we learn from *Aftonbladet* (December 3, 1971) that burglary in lovely Stockholm, "Venice of the North", has increased to such an extent that insurance companies have had to increase their rates for household insurance in the last two years from 48 to 125 kronor — close on threefold. Main cause of this increase in crime among people who are traditionally the most honest and most law-abiding in the world is given as drug addiction. People steal in order to feed the terrible craving.

Another report in the same issue of *Aftonbladet* begins with these words (translated, of course): "Policemen are fleeing from Stockholm". And so they are. Stockholm's police force, the newspaper tells us, is being decimated as policemen get out. The policeman who insist on getting out, we are told, are not lacking in fighting spirit because of the vicious assaults of which they are often the victims; their main reason for wanting to get out is that they don't want their children to grow up in the "brutal milieu" of the great city.

Another news reports tells of a 10-year-old schoolboy so tormented and repeatedly beaten black and blue by his "klasskamrater" that in the end his mother had to call in the police. The headmaster "visste inget" ("knew nothing") about what had been going on, in spite of repeated complaints.

Money and intellect between them have disvalued and eliminated from national life the elements of authority and discipline. These don't come from money or intellect but from an inherited learning laid up in the form of instinct and tradition. The money-intellect alliance must destroy authority because the *sine qua non* of authority is the subordination of money.

This is the secret of the present world-wide psychology of permissiveness. Haunted by the spectre of authority, which must prevail in the end, the money-intellect alliance must automatically come down every time on the side of those who rebel against any form of control.

MUSIC OF THE REVOLUTION

ONE of the most important historical facts of our times is that the working man has turned out, in all the circumstances of our modern industrial and commercial civilisation, to be rather untrustworthy revolutionary material. He has failed to live up to the expectations of Karl Marx and his comrades whose thinking was largely based on the appalling conditions among the working classes in the early days of industrialisation. Trade union activity has continued to improve the working man's standard of living, giving him an increasing stake in the *status quo* and therefore less and less willing to be used as revolutionary stormtroops.

Disoriented intellectuals in general and the young people in the universities in particular now form the main target area for revolutionary activity, the instrument used being a combination of music, drugs, sexual promiscuity and revolutionary ideology.

Among those who have commented on the relationship of rock music and the drug culture is Mr. Spiro Agnew, the Vice-President of the United States.

He was, however, labouring the only-too-obvious when he drew attention to folk-song lyrics containing words like "stoned", "grass" and "acid" as evidence of drug culture propaganda.

"There are millions of Americans," Mr. Agnew said, "who believe that if the music is loud enough, the distractions strong enough, the sedatives or stimulants active enough, they will drown out their frustrations and loneliness. By yielding to pressure to conform from their friends, they are creating a rigid establishment of their own, building an altar to alienation."

A South African churchman, Dr. H. G. van der Hoven, has explored the subject more deeply.

"Psychedelic music as inspired by the pop group The Beatles," he wrote, "represents a serious attack on youth, church and state and is an influence directly generated by Communism." He went on: "This cruel and satanic assault stems from a thorough scientific background resulting from research done by Pavlov, Luria and Platinov. We have to deal here with an aspect of the Cold War and this method is an excellent example of the so-called psychological warfare which is aimed at injuring our children's minds."

As was only to be expected, the Johannesburg *Sunday Times* quickly sprang to the defence of Beatle-type psychedelic music, condemned by Dr. van der Hoven.

The reply consisted of an interview with a way-out Catholic priest, Father Tony D'Alton, printed under a four-column heading which read: "Beatles Aren't Reds, Says Rand Priest".

"I'm afraid," said Father D'Alton, "that I must completely disagree. The idea that the Beatles could be Communist-inspired is ludicrous because they are capitalists of the highest order."

Father D'Alton defends Beatle music — but that does not mean necessarily that he is also Communist-inspired. As we pointed out before, we believe 99% of those involved in the promotion of Communist psychological warfare are not Communists at all but only Lenin's "useful idiots". In this category we place the Beatles and countless other exponents of psychedelic music, not to mention the poor fools who hold up these degraded characters as models for our young people.

Father D'Alton goes on to describe some of the lyrics in Beatle John Lennon's song *Imagine* as containing "the most beautiful thoughts I have ever come across" and he adds that some of these lyrics he has used "for meditation and for sermons in church." So, let us look at some of these lyrics which Father D'Alton finds so inspiring:

> *Imagine there's no heaven — it's easy if you try;*
> *No hell below us, above us only sky.*
> *Imagine all the people, living for today.*
> *Imagine there's no country — it isn't hard to do;*
> *Nothing to kill or die for — and no religion, too!*
> *Imagine all the people, living life in peace.*
> *Refrain :You may say that I'm a dreamer, but I'm not*
> *   the only one;*
> *I hope some day you'll join us and the world will live*
> *   as one.*
> *Imagine no possessions; I wonder if you can;*

No need for grief or hunger, a brotherhood of man.
Imagine all the people, sharing all the world;
Refrain: You may say that I'm a dreamer . . . etc.

Songs of this kind, combined with mildly hypnotic music and worked up into a form of mass hysteria, are a product of deep and clever psychological know-how, being designed to induce a form of alienation bordering on insanity.

The purpose, we may be sure, is to condition our young people for a future revolutionary role by arousing a mindless antagonism to the established authority and bringing about all those subtle changes which mark the difference between a living community and a mass or proletariat.

Let us, therefore, probe below the surface and consider how these results are produced.

Consciousness is always accompanied by a feeling of tension which may vary in intensity with the individual's ever-changing circumstances.

There are two possible attitudes towards this tension.

OPTION No. 1: The individual can accept the challenge of reality and learn to cope with tension, harnessing to life's purposes the contained energy. When this happens, we say that an individual is acquiring maturity. And an attitude which makes the individual exceptionally strong in coping with tension, giving him a sense of perfect security under stresses which would destroy others — such can only properly be called a religious attitude to life.

Indeed, that is the real purpose of a religion, as the great Oswald Spengler explains: "Religion is the personal relation to the powers of the world around us, expressed in a world view, in pious usages and the personal attitude of renunciation."

In short, this is one of the options. The individual can so strengthen and fortify himself that the tension that goes with consciousness ceases to be a problem.

OPTION No. 2: Then there is the other option. The individual can try to evade the burden of tension by seeking refuge in a totally unattainable world of make-believe. This is the psychology of Escapism. The individual becomes what Beatle John Lennon calls "a dreamer", a refugee from reality who tries to avoid all those personal responsibilities which increase the burden of tension.

Then, having failed to grapple with the problems of existence and still relentlessly pursued by the demon of tension, he is ready to seek relief in more drastic forms of escapism, including habit-forming drugs.

The Communist enemy reaches at our young people just at the time when, about to leave the sheltered environment of the parental home, they pause for a while between the two options.

With devilish cleverness, the enemy knows exactly what to do. First he must bring them all together in an atmosphere of group enthusiasm in which the identity of the individual is momentarily dissolved. This he does with mildly hypnotic music and dancing. Into this atmosphere, when the individual's defences are down, the enemy then insinuates the poison of the second option presented in a romantic and poetic light.

The lyrics which Father D'Alton likes so much is that poison in a highly concentrated form, a disastrously false attitude to life represented as exciting, "with it", and worthwhile.

As Spengler put it: "Utopian programmes are designed only for the spiritual bribery of the masses. The only serious intention is in the object of the bribery, the creation of a class as a fighting force by means of systematic demoralisation."

The whole idea is to create "masses" of disoriented individuals all passionately hostile towards a society which they blame for their inability to find happiness. These are now "class warriors" to be used in the streets by professional revolutionaries.

This is what Winston Churchill meant when he wrote of "this world-wide conspiracy for the overthrow of civilisation and for the reconstitution of society on the basis of arrested development, of envious malevolence and impossible equality".

"Arrested development" is precisely what is aimed at by those lyrics which Father D'Alton found so excitingly beautiful. He finds them "beautiful" because they flatter his own condition of disorientation, painting it in the false colours of some superior form of godliness.

What many parents don't know today is that the Communists themselves have frankly admitted that "acid-rock" music is meant to promote revolution. These damning admissions, however, are played down or totally excluded from the Liberal Establishment media of mass communication.

How many know that the film *Woodstock,* glorifying a great pop festival held at a place of that name in the United States was, and was meant by its producers to be highly sophisticated psychological warfare? The fact cannot be denied because the producer of the film has himself told us:

"In a sense we used the music because we selected most of the numbers for their political value; because they talk about marijuana, students, the generation gap, prejudice . . . We wanted to extract values from the music that went beyond the actual performance . . . What rock does provide is a sort of spiritual pick-me-up for the causes we believe in . . . With the footage we had we could have done almost anything. We could have made everybody appear completely stupid; we could have made the whole thing non-political. In fact what we did was to use every scene as a kind of political sales job."

The producer, Michael Wadleigh, made these statements in an interview with the Johannesburg *Sunday Times,* published on November 15, 1970. Wadleigh described as his favourite performance in the film the late Jimi Hendrix's abuse of the Star-spangled Banner. It was, he said, "a brilliant political statement — especially done by a black man with a head band, pierced ear lobes and everything else."

In *Rat,* a radical underground newspaper published in New York, the Woodstock festival was described as "the largest gathering of youth in the nation's history . . . a glimpse of Communism . . . First free dope territory in America. Three days of music and peace. And mud and acid (LSD), and hunger and thirst, and community and boredom. Containment-revolution."

But where is Woodstock? How did this place come to be the venue of "the largest gathering of youth in the nation's history"?

Reply: The venue for this "glimpse of Communism," as *Rat* describes it, was made available by Mr. Bernard Cornfield, the multi-millionaire financier whose world-wide Overseas Investment Service brought ruin to millions of small investors.

Is it pure coincidence too, that in May, 1921 the Communist Party of America was formed at Woodstock as a result of the fusion of two previously existing Communist groups?

J. Edgar Hoover, head of the Federal Bureau of Investigation (FBI), in his book *Masters of Deceit*, tells us that it was at the Woodstock meeting that the Communists formulated their plan for violent revolution, preparing "the workers for armed insurrection as the only means of overthrowing the capitalist state".

THE DRUG PUSHER

Children, tossed to and fro, and carried about with every wind of doctrine, by the sleight of men, and cunning craftiness, whereby they lie in wait to deceive.—Eph..4:14.

What is making American campuses the way they are? The newspapers are filled each day with stories about students on the rampage, bombing and burning university buildings, beating and being beaten up by the police. We only have to look at them when they appear in streets, even when they are not hurling rocks through shop windows, many of them bearded, long-haired and unwashed, to realise that somehow their minds have been tampered with.

How and by whom? One glance at a fairly typical American student newspaper provides a few clues. It is *The Daily Alestle,* newspaper of the Southern Illinois University at Edwardsville, just one of hundreds of American universities—by no means the best known and by no means the most notorious for student troubles.

Yale is far worse; Princeton still worse. Southern Illinois University pales into insignificance when compared with Harvard, whence proceeded such sinister figures as Felix Frankfurter, Alger Hiss, and a host of others who have been master-minding the Communist conspiracy in the United States since long before World War II.

Let us take one article from this student newspaper. It has the heading: "Treat Marijuana like Alcohol, recommends Law Professor" — the writer being John Kaplan, Professor of Law at Stanford University, who was employed by the California legislature to suggest revisions in the state's drug laws.

It seems that with Ronald Reagan in the Governor's chair, Professor Kaplan's recommendations were not accepted, but the learned investigator's findings have been published as a book, and the Southern Illinois University newspaper article was an extract from that book. Here we find a highly polished, highly sophisticated intellect being employed in the vile task of encouraging young people to "acquire an experience", "engage in a pleasant, safe rebellion". A sample paragraph:

> "Marijuana has become a symbol of the young in other ways as well. The effects of the drug — relaxation and euphoria — seem for some reason to be what this serious, intense and anxious generation most requires. Moreover, the young today are filled with a sense of distance from each other, a distance that they feel is somehow reduced while they sit around and share the effects of marijuana."

In writing all this, Professor John Kaplan can, of course, claim to be thoroughly objective because he is only stating the attitude of the drug's most articulate defenders. In the process, however, he supplies youth with a highly polished rationale for the vice, an explanation and justification of indulgence. In all that long article there is not one sentence to warn young people about the dangers of a drug which Stanford University's Professor Kaplan would like to see sold over the counter like alcoholic beverages.

What we find today on the campuses can only be described as an overthrow of American society on the battleground of the intellect. The American mind has been powerless to resist the attacks because they came not from outside where they could be recognised as alien and hostile, but from within, from people enjoying all the advantages of operating from a position of complete security.

How cleverly the hidden enemy adds fuel to the resentments of immaturity which, left alone, are part of the formative process of human nature!

Nowhere in such articles will students learn what are the real effects of drugs like marijuana, how they strike at the foundations of intellect and personality by disrupting the vital nexus between inner awareness and external reality.

Very few Americans today understand that a man like Professor Kaplan with a pen is a hundred times more destructive and dangerous to society than is a John Dillinger with his entire arsenal of firearms, or an Al Capone with his army of trigger-men and muscle-men.

What students are getting is a deadly cultural poison which neither they nor their parents recognise as poison—a poison designed not to kill, but only to paralyse into acquiescence and helplessness, a helplessness and acquiescence translatable into increased power for the conspirators.

The psychology of it is quite simple, when we know it.

A society like ours is held together by a form of group loyalty which is never stronger than when the group is being attacked by a plainly identifiable enemy.

Operations against such a society, conducted secretly from within, must necessarily take the form of weakening all these habitual, emotionally rooted bonds of group loyalty. In other words, as many as possible of the individuals of the society under attack must be detached or alienated from that society.

This process converts a "people" into a "mass" and can, therefore, be correctly described as "proletarianisation".

In every healthy society there is always a certain opposition of interests between the young, who take a fresh look at the world, and their elders who, for better or for worse, have already adjusted themselves to the world as it is. It is this little difference with their elders, a mere difference of phase in a healthy society, which the enemy does his best to intensify into mutual hatred and total alienation.

Shoulder-length hair and an intentionally slovenly appearance are encouraged and promoted precisely because they increase the tension between parents and children. And, of course, the encouragement of disorderly sexual conduct and the use of dagga and other drugs all contribute to the same end result.

Nothing could be more dangerously mistaken than to suppose that all these phenomena which loosen the bonds of society from within are separate and unrelated.

The last people in the world we should consult about the evils of dagga are our leftist university intellectuals who are already "hooked" by the drug of wildly unrealistic and spiritually escapist dreams of a state of society in which a shared euphoria will replace the trouble and strife which has marked the human story from the beginning of time.

Such people cannot be expected to know WHY a drug like dagga is far worse than tobacco or alcohol since such knowledge must inevitably play havoc with their whole system of sick ideas.

What these people need to know, but don't want to know, is that *there is no wholesome euphoria, no sound mental health and real happiness for the individual which is not built upon the foundations of a successful encounter with the realities of existence, and that there can be no escape from those realities — except an escape into the agonising nothingness of a condition of slavery.*

While it is true that alcohol and tobacco are harmful, it is equally true that both these evils against which the majority of people have acquired a certain degree of resistance or immunity, today stand between us and vastly more dangerous media of mood conditioning and escape.

Dagga strikes at those foundations, making easier and even attractive, an evasion of life's central challenge.

In a word, addiction to dagga or any other habit-forming drug, is totally irreconcileable with the building of a strong mind and personality equipped to deal with life's problems. Implicit in the habit is a dethronement of the will, a profound surrender of independence which reduces to nil any possibility of future resistance to forces which seek to set up a one-world state.

What sort of one-world state that would be, we do not have to wait to find out: the satanic methods being used tell us all we need to know.

Newspapers of the liberal establishment lose no opportunity of trying to create the impression that they are rendering an invaluable public service with sensational articles "exposing" the increasing prevalence of drug addiction, yet they muffle what they have to say on the subject with an ingenuity which borders on genius.

On the deeper issues involved in drug addiction, they fear the light worse than bedbugs. The reason for this is not hard to find: These journalists recognise the "drug sub-culture", as it has been called, as essentially a product of the Left, and they know with a sure instinct that they cannot attack drug addiction effectively without at the same time strengthening all those forces of human nature which stand opposed to their leftist brand of thinking.

In other words, "leftism" or "progressivism" or "liberalism" — call it what you like — is merely the political aspect of a cultural rootlessness which gives rise to a host of other socially pathological phenomena like "the permissive society" and everything that goes with it, including drug addiction.

It was only to be expected, therefore, that these same newspapers would give massive favourable publicity to a "music sub-culture" which is only the other side of the coin of the "drug sub-culture", both designed, somewhere down the line, to plant a yeasty rot in the will and spread further the contagion of rootlessness.

THE YOUTH REVOLT

YOUTH revolt is not a subject which can be fully dealt with under a single heading, since it is only one aspect of a revolutionary conspiracy which is world-wide, affecting everyone, including even the youngest schoolchildren.

Every chapter in this little book is relevant to the subject of the youth revolt.

Youth is today the target area of the most massive psychological warfare ever experienced by the human race. Lenin meant what he said: "We will undermine the youth of the West with sex and drugs."

Our young people are affected, no less than their elders by a debt-finance economic system which has produced a monstrous concentration of financial power in a few hands — and those not the cleanest.

Most of all are our young people affected by an undermining of the foundations of religious faith which has left millions searching desperately for some central insight which will restore to their lives a sense of purpose and direction.

Whereas the whole book is meant to be a message to youth, this chapter is meant only to bring the subject a little closer to them, whether they be on the university campus, in the classroom, or wherever they may be.

The whole of the Western World is seriously afflicted with student disorders and there are signs that the situation is going to be very much worse.

In the United States already students in hundreds of colleges have crossed that invisible line which forms the ultimate limit of legitimate protest and have become involved at what even their leaders frankly describe as "urban guerilla warfare".

Only the firmness of the South African Government has prevented the emergence of similar conditions in our universities, but the influences of anarchy and subversion are ever present and would promptly take advantage of any enlargement of the area of permissiveness.

These, then, are some of the questions which serious and thoughtful people are asking:

What is going on in the minds of our university students?

Why is it that university students provide revolutionary agitators with so much inflammatory human material?

The same questions could be asked about the teaching staffs in our universities, about church leaders, and about many others loosely described as "intellectuals", always remembering, however, that entire groups of people who qualify for the intellectual title give society no trouble whatsoever.

It stands to reason that if we know why some people who continuously employ their intellects give trouble while others do not, we shall be in a better position to unlock the riddle of what is happening in so many of our institutions of higher learning.

What we really want to know, with all our questions, is whether the trouble in the universities is a temporary social ailment or something which could be transformed into a revolutionary situation and civil war. In short: How dangerous is student revolt?

First of all, let us look at some of the disturbing facts of the last few years.

In the United States, campus protests against continued American involvement in the war against Communism in South East Asia resulted in a few months in the closing of 500 colleges, or about a third of the total number, the highlight of the disturbances being the shooting of four students at Kent Street College, Ohio, on May 4, 1970.

At hundreds of other colleges which were not shut down altogether an enormous amount of damage was done by rioting students, and lectures and seminars disrupted.

All this protest activity was brought to a focus in a mass gathering in Washington May 9 attended by an estimated 70,000 persons and addressed by leftist agitators, like Dr. Benjamin Spock and David Dellenger.

The sympathy of the mass media of communication both in South Africa and abroad being nearly always on the side of the protesters, it was inevitable that some of the important facts which would have helped us to understand what was happening in America were not reported, being regarded as not sufficiently newsworthy.

In South Africa we read a good deal about the shooting of four students at Kent State College, and, like millions of newspaper readers all over the world and more millions of television viewers, we saw the picture of one of the dead students lying on the ground with his girl friend stooping over him in a posture of shock and grief.

What we did not learn was that one month before the shooting the students at Kent College were addressed by one, Jerry Rubin, then under sentence to a prison term for his revolutionary activity along with six others at the 1968 Democratic Party Convention in Chicago. Rubin and his friends are on bail pending appeal and have been filling in the time addressing student audiences all over the United States.

Here are a few samples of the revolutionary fire-water which helped to turn the heads of the students and quickly converted "student protest" into "urban guerilla warfare":

> Until you people are prepared to kill your parents you aren't ready for the revolution . . . The American school system will be ended in two years. We are going to bring it down. Quit being students. Become criminals. We have to disrupt every institution and break every law. . . Do you people want a diploma or to take school over and use it for your own purposes? . . . It's quiet here now but things are going to start again.

This was reported at the time in the local newspaper, the *Akron Beacon Journal,* and later in the *New York Times.*

Speeches of this kind were delivered in March and April in scores of other colleges by comrades Jerry Rubin, Dave Dellenger and Abbie Hoffman, also convicted of inciting to riot at the Chicago Democratic Convention, the inflammatory theme being taken up by countless student leaders previously caught up in revolutionary fervour.

Here are extracts from some of the other speeches by Jerry Rubin, which the newspapers of the liberal establishment in most cases considered not sufficiently newsworthy:

> The war is not just in Asia or in the ghettos; it's on campuses. School imposes guilt — it's a pacification programme. Intellectuals are working for nothing. We can only succeed by breaking it down. If we close the universities we deliver a body blow to society. . . .

Don't go on an intellectual trip. This is a life trip.
I'm talking about life and death. Books should be
burned — they appress us. F—— history! Get stoned
and look to the future.

We are going to invade the schools and free our
brothers. We will burn the buildings and the books.
We will give brooms and pails to the administrators
so they can be useful and sweep the place up. Demonstrations on campuses aren't 'demonstrations' — they
are jail-breaks. Slave revolts. We can end this war —
we've got America on the run. We've combined youth,
music, sex, drugs and rebellion with treason — and
that's a combination hard to beat.

Also not reported abroad was the news that on Friday,
May 1, three days before the shooting, Kent College students,
well primed with alcohol and fighting talk, poured out of
student bars as on a signal and went on a rampage. On
this occasion five police officers and two students were
injured when a mob of 500 swept through downtown Kent
until the early hours of Saturday, taunting the police and
smashing shop windows.

Turning their attention to their own campus, they
burned down the Reserve Officer Training Corps (ROTC)
building and drove back the fire-fighters with stones after
slashing the fire hoses.

On Sunday night (May 3) there was another student-
police confrontation in which ten persons were injured and
62 arrested after the students had defied the dawn-to-dusk
curfew.

Contradictory accounts of the final clash in which four
students were shot have been supplied by different eye-
witnesses, but no one has denied that the National Guards,
thinly dispersed in the vicinity of the college buildings, were
set upon by a howling mob of students and that the guards,
having run out of tear-gas, were being assailed with stones
and pieces of iron when the shooting began.

What happened at Kent College is vitally important
to all of us, no matter where we live, because it is symptomatic of what is happening in universities all over the
Western World — and not only in universities.

Circumstances are the same and the causes at work
are the same, so that if we can correctly analyse and explain

what is happening at any one point we have the answer for all.

When many people in different places are ill, exhibiting the same symptoms, we only need to identify the virus in one case and we then know how to deal with an entire epidemic. It is much the same with the spiritual and intellectual sickness which today afflicts so many of our university intellectuals — the same set of symptoms, endlessly repeated, clearly indicating the same set of causes.

However sincerely many of these protesting students may feel about their agitation for a "better world", we may be sure they are being organised and exploited by a tiny minority of revolutionaries for purposes which have little or nothing to do with the motives which appear on the surface, the Communists themselves in Russia and elsewhere having so obviously failed in fifty years to produce anything remotely resembling that "ideal socialist state" which has become the intellectual lodestar of so many protesting and rioting students.

The role which students are expected to play in the great revolutionary struggle of our times was never more clearly stated than in a brochure put out by the University Christian Mission, an organisation with headquarters in Stellenbosch, South Africa:

> The proletariat, the 'workers' of pre-revolutionary Europe, have had their day. They are a spent force with regard to social change, without identity or true political potential. The new orthodoxy of the unions reigns supreme; the workers have their work — and that is all they appear to want. A little more money, a strike here and there.
>
> Nevertheless it is not simply the case that the revolutionary forces which first revealed themselves to the world at the beginning of the century in the fantastic phenomenon of Marxism are spent. Rather is it true to say that they have passed into the hands of a new section of society . . .
>
> A new figure has stepped out into the political arena of the world, a new force has revealed itself that cannot be ignored: it is the power of the student community — Student Power.

The big question, then, is whether a revolutionary

overthrow of the existing order can be achieved by means
of the student movement. Could the American student
revolt develop into large-scale urban guerilla warfare and
create the anarchy that must necessarily precede an overthrow of the existing order?

Part of the answer is supplied in the UCM brochure:
"The 'workers' have had their day. They are a spent force
with regard to social change . . . the new orthodoxy of the
unions reigns supreme; the workers have their work and
that is all they appear to want".

The correctness of this analysis could hardly have been
more vividly demonstrated than in New York on May 8, 1970
when 500 construction workers stormed the Memorial Hall
in Wall Street after Mayor Lindsay had lowered the *Stars
and Stripes* to half-mast in honour of the four slain Kent
State University students. The helmeted workers, reports the
New York Daily News, "left a trail of blood and bruises"
as they broke up an anti-war rally of an equal number of
student demonstrators.

The presence of the student protesters, many of them
long-haired, unwashed and in hippy attire, had all the
appearance of having been carefully organised; the workers,
on the other hand, just happened to be employed on a
nearby construction site and were having their lunch when
their attention was caught by the anti-war demonstrators
and the city hall flag flying at half-mast.

What all this means, considered as a sample of the
mood of the American working classes in general, is that the
worker is not nearly so easily ignited into a state of
revolutionary fervour as the students and other intellectuals;
therefore, it is extremely doubtful whether a full-scale
revolutionary situation can be created, in all the present
circumstances, using inflamed intellectuals alone.

The whole history of Communist revolution shows
clearly enough that the management of revolution must
always be in the hands of intellectuals, but that their
main task has been that of converting the working masses
into a battering ram capable of overthrowing the existing
political authorities. The revolutionary intellectual is not
the revolution; he is only the ferment; and his own revolt
must come to nothing unless he can communicate it to the
workers, the only people who can gather enough mass and

momentum to overthrow the existing order.

So that attempts to answer one of our questions: How dangerous is student revolt? — only dangerous to the degree that it can foment worker-revolt.

Now we come to the other questions: Why are students and certain other intellectuals so easily made into the agents and instruments of revolution? What goes on in their heads? Is something wrong? Why are some classes of intellectuals totally resistant to subversive influences?

Even those who know would be at their wits end to compress answers to such questions into a few sentences which anyone can understand.

All we can hope to do within the compass of a short article is to apply a magnifying glass, as it were, to one small but important aspect of a highly complex problem.

There is mature intellectual activity and there is immature.

Mental activity is mature, furthering the true ends of life, when it is intimately related to action and is being continuously tested by results, or is the fruit of real experience.

People like engineers and medical doctors, to take only two examples at random, live in this kind of mental world, which explains why they do not figure very prominently among revolutionary intellectuals. They employ intellect but they know its limitations, working as they do constantly under the sharp and laborious discipline of knowing that even the most vividly delineated idea or notion can be dangerously wrong or, at any rate, incapable of being implemented.

They have learned from experience, and are never allowed to forget, that the concepts or symbols which we use in all our abstract thinking correspond only approximately with the realities they are supposed to represent.

However lifelike, rounded and complete these symbols may seem to be as we use them, they are, after all, only shadows or silhouettes, omitting in many cases much more than they contain. And it goes without saying that our thought processes, untutored by long experience, are never more dangerously inadequate than when we speculate about people and political institutions.

Even in some elementary process of thinking, like the planning of a chicken run, any person lacking real experience of such work is liable to find his visualisations and proportions woefully insufficient when he tries to translate them into actuality.

In short, mature intellectual activity is always attended by a humility which recognises the mind's inherent fallibility.

Immature brain-spinners and inventors of ideal worlds we have always had with us, but never perhaps in such numbers as in today's world of fragmentation and specialisation, made worse by a type of university education which does not educate for life but rather for economic function.

With most people immaturity is only a passing phase, the immaturity of youth and inexperience, which disappears as soon as they come to grips with life and have to make decisions which produce immediate personal consequences. Then intellect is cut down to size and they find themselves confined more and more to the solution of problems which lie within their range.

The others continue to enjoy, all their lives, the "freedom" of undisciplined thinking, being permitted to do so by the peculiar circumstances of their existence; and so they go on producing in the little picture-box of their minds an exciting architecture of ideas, quite admirable from a literary point of view, in which all the problems which have baffled mankind down the ages are solved with marvellous ease.

The propagation of such ideas then becomes for them a goal in life, imparting a spurious, mirage-like sense of direction that acquires religious overtones and gives rise to a dangerous unregulated zeal or fanaticism and places at the service of false notions some of the finest qualities of human nature, like compassion, courage and determination.

The Greeks had a word for it: *hubris,* the arrogance of an intellect which has not been reduced to a proper state of submission to the Total Actuality.

Thinking which is not answerable for results is always sterile. It can make nothing and produce nothing — not even a revolution. But it is a kind of thinking, much concentrated these days in our universities and churches, which can be organised and exploited by the real promoters of revolution, the deadly realists, the hard-core Communists, the Jerry Rubins and Abbie Hoffmans, and the bigger plotters who remain always in the shadows.

These men do not believe the slogans; they use them.

And they never lose sight of the real goal — power for themselves, a world which they will control.

SCHOLAR POWER

Many people are afflicted with a kind of pathological unwillingness to detect any sort of plan or sinister motive behind a wide variety of disturbing social phenomena. They are warned by something at the back of their minds that if they find such a plan or motive, then they are going to feel under an obligation to do something about it. And that, of course, means an increase of responsibility and tension!

So, they prefer to keep their minds closed for fear of discovering the disturbing truth.

Recently there appeared in the South African newspapers reports about a pamphlet being circulated in South African schools, ostensibly issued by a group of scholars who identify themselves as "The Schools Action Committee", with a Johannesburg Post Office box number as their only address. As one newspaper tells us, the pamphlet "urges scholars all over South Africa to unite against the power of 'grown-ups' and work for change in schools". If a teacher addresses them by their first names, they are told, they have a perfect right to address him also by his first name.

Needless to say, the newspapers have accepted this little exercise in "scholar power" at face value as something spontaneously generated among a group of schoolchildren. A study of the complete circular, running into four closely typed foolscap pages, disposes of any idea that this is a product of juvenile minds; and anyone who has followed the progress of similar exercises abroad, especially in the United States and United Kingdom, cannot doubt for a moment that it is an inseparable part of what Dr. van der Hoven described as "a satanic attack on youth, church and state".

Like Beatle-type music and the promotion of drug addiction, we see this attempt to stir up antagonism between scholar and teacher as portion of a vast spider-web of cultural, religious and political subversion. In the United Kingdom the same "scholar power" conspiracy, master-minded by extremely clever leftist operators who employ criminality as a political weapon, has made tremendous progress, with results that are already plainly apparent. I consider only a few items of news from Britain under this heading:

● *Evening Standard*, 16.2.72: DOSSIER OF CLASS-ROOM VIOLENCE—A teacher's leg was broken by a pupil who kicked him. Another teacher was hit over the head with a milk bottle by an angry parent and another was seriously assaulted by 17 and 18-year-old ex-pupils who came back to school to attack him. These are some of the 52 cases of school violence collected by the National Association of Schoolmasters and published today in a special report. . .

● *Evening Standard*, 30.12.71: A teacher was threatened with rape by a father whose son had been kept late at school; another was kicked in the groin by a 15-year-old boy; yet another had to punch a violent student on the chin. . .

● *The Guardian*, 5.1.72: Mr. Terry Casey who last week criticised some 'cowardly' head teachers for their attitude to school violence has now accused many teachers of deliberately trying to play down the problem of discipline.

● *Sunday Telegraph*, 28.11.71: Traditional schoolboy fisticuffs have given way to terror by thugs in primary and secondary schools throughout Great Britain, according to leading educationists. Thousands of teachers say they face a vicious blackboard jungle in which violence is increasing term by term and 'honour' is an ugly word.

"Scholar Power" in Britain has taken the form of groups of schoolchildren, including one called "Children's Angry Brigade" which prints a "communique" in a magazine called *Children's Rights*, saying:

"Unscrew locks, smash tannoys, paint blackboards red, grind all the chalk to dust. All sabotage is effective in hierarchical systems like schools. You're angry — you know what to do".

Can anyone seriously believe that the printing and publication of a sophisticated magazine and the distribution of 5,000 copies in British schools, not to mention the wording of the vandalism communiques, can all be attributed to juvenile enterprise and invention?

We only have to look at the situation in British schools to know what certain underground criminals of the Left would like to do with South African schools — indeed, what they have already begun to do!

When once we recognise the conspiratorial nature of these activities, all designed to create anarchy and proletarianise populations in preparation for some hoped-for revolutionary overthrow of all existing authority, we then have a key which immediately explains a host of other phenomena obviously designed to promote the same purposes.

EXAMPLE TO YOUTH

The whole world can learn from one nation which has succeeded to an astonishing degree in insulating its young people against influences which are causing havoc all over the western world.

There is sometimes a whole world of hidden meaning in some small item in the newspapers which most people would not even read beyond the first few lines. Here is an example from a South African morning newspaper:

> The Jewish-Zionist youth movement in South Africa, the Ichud Habonim, celebrates its 40th anniversary this month (September, 1970). The organisation runs youth camps throughout the country, including the largest such camp in South Africa, at Onrus in the Cape, where 1,200 youngsters spend three weeks under canvas each year. To celebrate its 40th anniversary it has organised a variety of activities at national and local levels. Part of the Durban celebrations will include a preview of the Israeli film *War after the War*.

How many South Africans have ever heard of Ichud Habonim and the splendid work it has been doing down the years for the sons and daughters of the Jewish community? Very few, we may be sure. Indeed, it needed a 40th anniversary celebration even to get this powerful youth movement a brief reference in a provincial daily newspaper under a modest heading.

Yet here we have a South African organisation, a replica of similar organisations all over the Western world, which provides the total answer to what has become for most parents one of the most worrying problems of our times — the disorientation of modern youth, giving rise to such ugly symptoms as hippy lawlessness, campus violence and drug-taking.

We only have to study Ichud Habonim to find out precisely what our young people need and must have if their personalities are to be stabilised and enriched with a sense of direction and purpose.

They must feel that they belong to a community with identity, a community with a history and a mission which makes all those who belong to it feel somehow different, binding them together in a shared enthusiasm making life significant and worthwhile.

What it all adds up to is a nationalism which supplies the individual with a set of purposes vastly more important than his tiny self, liberating energies of the heart and mind that can be freed in no other way.

We can imagine the bright-eyed eagerness with which the young men and women of Ichud Habonim watched the preview of that film *War after the War*, feeling as they saw it part of a great world-shaping drama.

There is no more intense nationalism today than that of the Jewish people, who, in a world of dissolving values, enjoy the immense advantage of nationalism whose frontiers are in the mind and not on the ground.

Israel is often described as a Jewish homeland. It was so described in the Balfour Declaration. It is, of course, nothing of the kind. No one has ever suggested that all the world's Jews will return there (and even the language of Bible prophecy admits of only a tiny minority). Not one Jew in a thousand now living in the diaspora wants to go and live in Israel. But all are passionately devoted, often at considerable personal cost to themselves, to defend this barren strip of territory.

Israel's importance is purely symbolical, pegging at one point on the earth's surface (strategically the most important), and intensifying to near fanaticism a nationalism of the mind.

Here we have a nationalism which sets the whole world by the ears, claiming as its own a country in which it does not want to live, a country useful only as a pivot or pressure point for a power which is world-wide in its sources and its reach.

Mr. David Ben-Gurion, the former Prime Minister of Israel, has said at much:

> The state of Israel is part of the Middle East only in geography which is, in the main, a static element. From the decisive aspects of dynamism, creation and growth, Israel is part of World Jewry. *Rebirth and Destiny of Israel,* page 489.)

Made to feel part of a nation which has come a long way and knows where it is going, Jewish youth remains impervious to influences which are demoralising millions of young Gentiles all over the Western world, making them "a reproach and a hissing", and shock troops of anarchy and revolution.

Recently an estimated 150,000 boys and girls from many European countries gathered on the Isle of Wight for an orgy of permissiveness, all engulfed in a shared paranoia and drawn unresisting, like so many lemmings, towards their own destruction.

How many Jewish boys and girls were to be found in this dirty, untidy, pot-smoking, drug-taking, copulating multitude? No count was made, but it is the safest guess in the world, backed by experience all over the world, that there were very few, if any.

(This article about Ichud Habonim was reprinted, verbatim and without comment by the South African Zionist Record.)

THE RACE ISSUE AS A WEAPON IN MIND WARFARE

ANOTHER major weapon of the Communist conspiracy, equal in importance to the Marxist-Fabian socialist ideology, is the race issue.

Indeed, the two are complementary — just like the open, inviting gateway and the barking shepherd dogs which steer a flock of sheep into an enclosure.

People are first shown what looks like a most attractive "way out" of all their present difficulties; and then they must be frightened and pushed into accepting so drastic a change in their way of life.

In other words our present democratic system, based on private ownership and private enterprise, must be shaken to pieces with internal conflict, mounting crime and insupportable taxation before people can be expected to consider Socialism as an attractive alternative.

And the race issue has been found to be by far the most effective means of shaking a social system to pieces and demoralising a population — provided, of course, that the country concerned already has some sort of race problem which can be exploited for this purpose.

The United States, with its 12,000,000 Negroes and other maladjusted minority groups was ready made for the employment of this thoroughly heartless form of psycho-political warfare.

Britain did not have a race problem. Therefore one had to be imported, with all the unpleasant social consequences now being experienced in the larger population centres.

The Australians are still without a race problem worth mentioning, but they will not remain long in this happy situation if present massive efforts to overthrow their country's traditional "White Australia" immigration policy are permitted to succeed.

Just how the race issue is being used in efforts to shake to pieces the existing free enterprise system and disrupt all those psychological bonds which hold people together in a living community, is explained in the following chapters.

Here again there can be no victory that does not begin on the battleground of the mind.

Our only possible defence is to know what our enemy is trying to do to us. When we know that, our defence on that front is impregnable.

It is not enough to know that the enemy is using the race issue as a weapon of psycho-political warfare. We also need to know exactly how it is being used.

And that means knowing more about the mind and instincts of man and being able to see for ourselves how these can be manipulated. If the enemy is clever, then we must be just as clever, or even cleverer, or else he shall be.

The key to the entire mystery will be found in what has been called the *Equality Dogma* which insists that there are no differences between the various races of man except those purely superficial ones like the skin colour, etc., and other differences which can all be traced to environmental influences.

If this theory is correct, it stands to reason that racial discrimination is both unnecessary and wholly unjust, and that any failure on the part of one group to enjoy the same success as another must be the result of some form of oppression.

All One-World socialist propaganda, subversion and other forms of pressure rest on this narrow foundation of belief like a huge inverted pyramid.

We can therefore understand why this narrow foundation of belief, the Great Lie of the 20th Century, is defended with furious zeal — and why it is seldom, if ever, exposed to the perils of genuine debate.

If races are inherently different and need for their fulfilment and happiness different life-styles, then it also stands to reason that the last thing they would want is a highly centralised world government which denies or ignores these differences.

What each race will then want and need is a form of government as close to itself as possible, with rulers who can be easily replaced when necessary.

The race issue does not only divide a community against itself, setting one group in burning enmity towards another; it can also divide an otherwise homogeneous group, destroying its natural inner cohesion; in very many cases it

even plants division inside the mind of the individual,
dividing him against himself and leaving him confused and
unable to decide what attitude to adopt over an issue which
affects him so closely.

All this the race issue does by exploiting a universal
and deeply-felt human need — the need for a sense of
belonging, a sense of community.

Man is essentially a social animal, requiring for his
fulfilment and the unfolding of his inner potentialities, a
relatively homogeneous human environment. He needs to
be with people like himself, people who speak the same
language, share the same values and standards and life-style
and even laugh at the same jokes.

How is this deep and totally inescapable need to be
satisfied in a world where, under the influence of industrial
and commercial development, people of different race are
being brought increasingly into close juxtaposition?

There are only two ways possible.

If the equality dogma is correct, if all races are exactly
the same except for purely superficial differences, the
obvious answer is to find that sense of community and
belonging inside all mankind considered as a single group.

If, on the other hand, the equality dogma is false—
which it most certainly is—then the individual has no hope
of ever finding personal fulfilment and happiness except
inside a smaller homogeneous group which takes full cog-
nisance of a reality of difference which has persisted from
the beginning of time and which no one has ever been able
to change.

SCIENCE FALSIFIED

For many years a heavy blanket of falsification and
silence has been laid on the racial aspects of genetics and
anthropology. The scientist mainly responsible for the
falsification was one Professor Franz Boas, of Yale University, born in Russia, who supplied the Establishment with
"proofs" that there are no inherent racial differences and
that environment, not heredity, must be called upon to
explain differences which are too obvious to be denied.

Scores of honest scientists have been smeared and
hounded out of their jobs for insisting that inherent racial
differences do exist, and so well have the persecutors suc-

ceeded that today honest anthropology and genetics are virtually "underground" sciences.

Imagine the horror then, when at a meeting of the National Academy of Science in Washington, early in May, 1970, a scientist with an unassailable record nailed his flag to the mast and challenged the Academy to investigate genetic differences in the intelligence of white and Negro!

The challenger was Professor William Shockley, of Stanford University, who happens not even to be a geneticist or anthropologist. He is a Nobel Prize winning physicist, world-famous for his work on transistors. Drawing attention to tests which had indicated genetic differences in intelligence, Professor Shockley summed as follows:

> If the difficulty of the black minority is a basic difference in the genetic potential for developing the capacities needed to approach parity in a modern technological society, and if this disparity is indeed becoming worse in each generation . . . then failure to attempt to diagnose is . . a profound irresponsibility.

Professor Shockley has now greatly strengthened the position on another hero of science, Professor Arthur Jensen, a psychologist of Berkeley University.

The American magazine *Newsweek* remarks: "Together, the pair have been constant thorns in the academy's decidedly thin skin for a long time."

Academicians loyal to the Establishment have done everything in their power to prevent a thorough investigation of racial differences. The National Academy of Science was made to "face the problem", but declined to take any steps to investigate it.

What does that mean except that they know what the results of such an investigation would be, and they are afraid that the scientific truth would have too many disturbing implications?

The subject of racial differences was discussed by Dr. Robert Gayre of Gayre, editor of *Mankind Quarterly,* when he addressed the National Forum in Durban in March, 1971.

Dr. Gare declared that all racial tension can be traced to one basic cause: attempts at integrating widely divergent races. In this way it is efforts to suppress race consciousness which produce the worst manifestation of animosity between the races.

Dr. Gayre came into some prominence in Britain when he appeared as an expert witness in a case at Lewes when the author of a pamphlet entitled *The Great Multiracial Fraud Exposed* was prosecuted under the Race Relations Act of 1965 on the ground that the pamphlet was an insult" to coloured people in Britain and was calculated to exacerbate race relations.

He dealt in particular with the use of the word feckless" to describe the Negro character.

Said Dr. Gayre: "It is a Scottish word meaning inconsequential to inefficient. Anyone acquainted with negroid races all over the world know it to be true, if we judge them by our standards, as they prefer their leisure to the dynamism which the white and yellow races show, and so make very little effort to compete in labour or efficiency or in the creation of projects."

The general tenor of the article which formed the basis of the prosecution was an analysis of the theories of Frans Boas, a German-born biologist who emigrated to the USA and extended his activities to anthropology between 1890 and the 1930's. The article sought to prove that the Boas theories of race and multiracialism are a deception and are closely related to Communist dogma. Here are only a few paragraphs from Dr. Gayre's masterly analysis of the Boas doctrine:

> Boas was not an anthropologist, but a politico-philosophical-sociological thinker, who in a vacuum began to propound what were in fact political concepts under the guise of social anthropology.
>
> In order to give some 'biological' basis to his doctrines he propounded what were in fact the completely discredited the doctrines of Lamarck. In the effort to do so, he had to show that the environment could completely change the type.
>
> One of his most preposterous claims was that the American White were becoming steadily Red Indian in type, owing to the influence of the American environment! Such complete nonsense was laughed out of court by all responsible scientists.
>
> However, since his doctrines were those which were essential for the Left direction in politics, of a

Communist nature, they attracted to his school of thought many politically-inclined sociologists who became 'social anthropologists', some claiming to be anthropologists.

The White, said Dr. Gayre, is not consistently, in all features, superior to the Negroid; but in those factors which have characterised the European type of civilisation (dynamism, inventiveness, the ability to think three-dimensionally, acquisitiveness, foresight, and so on), the White and Yellow stocks are markedly ahead of the average of the Negroid.

After the judge's summing-up, the jury returned a unanimous verdict of "Not guilty", thus establishing the principal that the relevant section of the Act cannot be enforced if alleged "insults" reflect fact.

After giving evidence, Dr. Gayre was viciously attacked in the Press and was forced on several occasions to defend himself by bringing libel actions against his detractors. It is highly significant, however, that no one claiming any status as a biologist or anthropologist, ever dared to accept his challenge to debate these issues of racial differences.

THE EQUALITY DOGMA

South Africa's newspaper-reading public is exposed daily to a continuous barrage of propaganda designed to undermine its morale by planting a sense of guilt over the country's traditional policy of racial separation.

A good example of this form of brainwashing was an article which occupied most of the first page of the magazine supplement of the Argus Company's *Sunday Tribune* under the heading WHITE IS BRIGHT, the message being that Blacks would also be "bright" if they enjoyed the same environmental advantages, and could even be expected to duplicate the "economic miracle" of modern Japan. The article was illustrated with a picture of Black babies squatting in a typical slum backyard.

Behind all this leftist brainwashing on the subject of race there is an intellectual dishonesty which people who know the truth about race must find utterly revolting.

By intellectual dishonesty, we do not mean a fully conscious intention to deceive; we refer to a form of willing

...ll deception which makes its victims ideal instruments for
the propagation of dangerously misleading falsehoods which
certain power-wielders find politically advantageous. This
willingness to be deceived on the subject of race can be
explained in two ways:

1. The false doctrine of racial equality happens to
flatter an attitude to life now prevalent among the rootless
intellectuals all over the Western world.

2. Men's beliefs are inevitably influenced by all the
obvious personal advantages of alignment with Establishment
thinking.

In the same way that the discoveries of Galileo
threatened the anthropocentric cosmogony of his time, so
the findings of a true race science conflict with the basic
requirements of ever-increasing centralisation of political
power culminating in some form of one-world government.

Equally revolting are the efforts of the newspapers to
dress up as genuine debate exercises in propaganda in which
the opposite point of view is feebly represented or excluded
altogether.

Lacking the space for a thorough examination of the
race-equality dogma, we must content ourselves with a few
comments on the *Sunday Tribune* article.

To start with, who is this "Dr. Gerald Machanik" who
"poses a question to make South Africans think"? What
are his qualifications for pontificating so confidently on this
subject? Is he an anthropologist? Has he any scientific
educational background at all? We are told nothing.

In the article, however, several names are mentioned
and Dr. Machanik does not omit to tell us that "The verdict
of science was pronounced in a UNESCO statement issued
in 1962 by 14 famous scientists including Professors Julian
Huxley, J. B. S. Haldane, Solly Zuckerman and Ashley
Montagu", their findings being summed up in this sentence:
"No basis exists for believing that groups of mankind differ
in their innate capacity for intellectual and emotional development."

The most active of these UNESCO spokesmen is Ashley
Montagu, who has written scores of books and magazine
articles and has appeared in countless radio and television
programmes popularising the notion that there are no basic
racial differences except those which appear upon the

surface. We remember that on one occasion when he was being interviewed on television he became very angry when questioned about his original name; whatever that was, it was not Ashley Montagu. Usually, however, Professor Montagu runs little risk of being asked embarrassing questions by liberal establishment interviewers.

Professor Ashley Montagu helps to explain the saying made famous by George Orwell in *Animal Farm,* that "all animals are equal but some animals are more equal than others". What he did was to lend his name to a full-page advertisement in the *New York Times* of January 5, 1970, recommending a book by Professor Ernest van den Haag, entitled *The Jewish Mystique* in which it is argued that the Jews are a master race with a superior intellectual apparatus.

Another book, *The Creative Elite* by Dr. Nathaniel Weyl, also claiming that the Jews are an intellectually superior race, has likewise never been challenged by liberal establishment anthropologists, who spend so much of their time insisting that all races are equal.

What an interesting article the *Sunday Tribune* could have if it would quote some of the acknowledged experts who have so easily demolished the race-equality dogma as enunciated by the likes of Montagu, Klineberg, Herskowitz, Ruth Benedict, Isador Chein, Dobzhansky, Weltfish and the Negro psychologist Kenneth Clark!

The unwelcome truth is that all this high-powered "anti-racism" is nothing more than an inverted minority racism which has been reduced to the necessity of falsifying a whole range of sciences which have to do with the task of explaining man to himself — anthropology, genetics, psychology, etc., etc.

Robert Ardrey in his book *The Social Contract* quotes what he describes as "a most revealing example of what passes for science" from Professor Sol Tax's introduction to a series of articles by some of the more vigorous of his young promoters of the race-equality dogma:

> We particularly abhor the misuse by bigots or politicians of any of our knowledge. As scientists we never know all the truth; we must grope and probe and ever learn; but we know infinitely more than the glib racists — whether in the United States or South Africa. We are equalitarians, not because we can prove

absolute equality, but because we know absolutely that whatever differences there may be among large populations have no significance for the policies of nations. This comes from our knowledge of anthropologists; but it also pleases us as citizens of the world.

The devious ingenuity with which Professor Sol Tax makes out a case for a science "that pleases us as citizens of the world" proves one thing, if it proves nothing else: Sol Tax at any rate knows the truth about race and is not one of the self-deceived.

The article which the *Sunday Tribune* printed in its issue of March 12 gives the reader no clue to the existence of a massive and highly authoritative literature challenging the case for "race equality".

Professor Carleton Coon, author of the massive *Races of Man* and former president of the American Association of Physical Anthropologists, was almost driven out of his mind by a smear campaign, all originating in minority power sources, for daring to point to the evidence of a time lag in the emergence of the Negro race from the pre-sapiens state.

Other world-famous scientists who have qualified for the smear title of "racial bigots" etc., include Professor Henry Garrett, former Professor of Psychology at Columbia University, Sir Arthur Keith, former President of the British Association for the Advancement of Science, and more recently Professor William Shockley (Nobel Prize winner) and Professor Arthur Jensen, who were made the target of the most shocking abuse for daring to suggest at a meeting of the National Academy of Sciences in the U.S.A. that serious attention should be given to the subject of racial differences of intelligence in view of the great danger of rearing political policies on a foundation of scientific falsehood.

Minority racism is a *right-hand* glove on the hand that wears it; pulled off and exhibited inside-out it is a *left-hand* glove of anti-racism and anti-nationalism. How easily people are deceived by this shallow trick of psychological warfare designed to confuse us and prevent us from taking those steps which are necessary to ensure our national, racial and religious survival!

We cannot conclude this piece on the subject of race

without dealing briefly with a point only briefly mentioned above — the claim by Van den Haag (supported by Ashley Montagu and Nathaniel Weyl) that the Jews are a master race with an innately superior intellectual apparatus.

While it is undoubtedly true that Jews as a group enjoy competitive superiority in an urban, cosmopolitan environment, much of this superiority can be traced to the enormous advantage of mutual support arising out of intense race consciousness and the shared loyalty of a nationalism which is all the more intense for being geographically dispersed.

In other words, the Jew is racially strong in an environment which makes others racially weak.

There is a vast difference, too, between the kind of intelligence which gives one individual more money or power in the highly competitive environment of a great city and that other kind of intelligence which contributes every gain it makes to some shared cultural heritage, making possible splendours of achievement like the music of Mozart and Beethoven, the painting of Raphael and Rembrandt and the sculpture of Michelangelo, in which the great artist did little more than recapitulate and render complete works of creative imagination which may have required the lifelong efforts of successive generations of men.
to a status only "a little lower than the angels", that was so magnificently demonstrated in that period of history known as the Renaissance.

It was this kind of excellence, raising man momentarily

CRUCIFYING THE BLACK MAN

Men like Mr. Ramsey Clark (former U.S. Attorney-General) have an astonishing capacity for ignoring the facts which do not fit in with their own long-range political purposes, and of grossly misinterpreting awkward facts that cannot be overlooked.

How much the former U.S. Attorney-General must somehow contrive not to see and not to know before coming to South Africa to preach to us about race relations!

Questioned about the riots of a few years ago in the Watts district of Los Angeles, the only explanation he could think of was that social services in that area were inferior. What has happened there is that an excellent middle-class

residential district has been quickly converted into a seething
cauldron of filfth, anarchy and crime since the Blacks moved
in and the Whites moved out.

This has happened not because it is in the nature of the
Negroes to live like that, but only because their whole life
pattern has been disrupted and they have been prevented
from fulfilling themselves and organising themselves as an
ethnic entity. Conditions like those to be seen in Watts are
certainly not to be found in the villages of West Africa
whence came the forbears of most of America's Negroes and
where the people contrived to live happy and orderly lives
on a very much lower economic level.

The unhappy Negroes of the United States of America
are the casualties of one of the biggest and most damaging
lies of the century — the lie of racial equality, the Big Lie
which forms the foundation stone of One-World propaganda.

Things are happening all over the United States which
present the same picture and teach the same lesson — except
to those who don't want to know. Let us consider one out-
standing example which permits of no other explanation
except the obvious one that the Negro is incapable of
reproducing the White man's social and environmental
patterns: the Pruit-Igoe residential complex at St. Louis.

Millions of dollars were spent in 1959 in building a
vast complex of 43 11-storey apartment houses on a 55-acre
patch of what was formerly the Kerry Patch slum. Never
before had so much money been spent on a single project
aimed at creating a multi-racial paradise for people in the
middle and lower income groups.

Being in conflict with the realities of human nature, the
plan did not work out as expected. To start with, no Whites
would move into these marvellous buildings set in lovely
grounds. So Pruit-Igoe was all-Black from the beginning.

The long sad story is told by Dan Smoot in the March
17, 1971, issue of *Review of the News* (Belmont, Mass.,
U.S.A.). Pruit-Igoe has been reduced to an area of almost
total anarchy. Of the 43 "high-rise" apartment houses,
buildings which were meant to accommodate 11,498 people,
only 14 are now occupied. The other 29 are being fenced
off to prevent further vandalism, and it has been estimated
that it would cost 39 million dollars to restore all the
buildings.

An urban renewal dream was converted in fifteen years

into what Smoot describes as "a cancer in the heart of St. Louis, an indescribable cesspool of filth, fear and crime. Vandals kept elevators out of order most of the time. Stairs, landings, halls, yards, playgrounds, open spaces, recreation rooms and elevators, reeked of human offal and were littered with garbage, beer cans, broken wine bottles, assorted trash. Rape, robbery and assault — in the buildings and on the grounds — were commonplace . . . The laundry galleries (occupying three floors in every block) were taken over by hoodlums . . . where men and women drank, gambled, fought and engaged in sexual acts in full view of the playing children . . . Stores would not make any deliveries to Pruit-Igoe and taxicabs would not go there. Even the police gave up . . . Repairs were ripped out as fast as they could be made . . ."

Things like this are happening all over the United States — we saw it again, not because the Negro is basically incapable of living a clean, well ordered life but only because he is even less successful than the White man in adapting himself to a modern, industrialised, highly competitive, megalopolitan society with all its unnatural pressures and temptations. Meanwhile, unscrupulous politicians — or, rather the power-wielders behind the politicians — flatter the Negro and pamper him while they exploit him for his vote in a country where power goes automatically to those who can organise the various minority groups into a voting majority.

Thus we find the huge tax-free foundations like the Ford Foundation and the Carnegie Foundation spending millions of dollars getting the Negroes to register as voters —which most of them would never bother to do if left to their own devices.

The degraded condition in which the Negro lives in the United States is only part of the price he pays for all this pampering and bribery.

A Washington report from Jeremy Campbell to the London *Evening Standard* tells us that "a great husband shortage is raging across the length and breadth of Black America, playing havoc with normal sexual roles, undermining family life and prompting a rash of ominous warnings of new upheavals to come in the urban slums".

According to Dr. Lee Rainwater of Harvard University, more than one million Negro women cannot find men to marry, 10% of all Black births are illegitimate and one-third of all Negro homes are without fathers.

Says Dr. Rainwater: "The Negro family in America is not stabilising. It is deteriorating at an increasingly rapid rate. The drive and incentive of the Black male is being destroyed by the dominance of the female and his dependence on the welfare system".

Dr. Jacqueline Jackson, a Negro sociologist of Duke University, declares that more than one million Negro men of marriageable age "have, for all intents and purposes, vanished from the American scene". She says they are dying earlier as victims of pulmonary tuberculosis, accidents of all kinds, homicide, drug overdoses, alcoholism, insanity and suicide.

Other Negroes have helped to swell America's enormous prison population. Non-Whites comprise only 12.5% of the population but make up 50% of the nation's prison inmates, and in some city jails the figure is as high as 80%.

Other investigators claim that it would be nearer the truth to say that 90% of Negro homes lack a "father" or "husband", the man present in very many cases being only a temporary sojourner. In fact, the Negro in the United States is simply not reproducing the White man's traditional family pattern.

Needless to say, liberal establishment propaganda blames the American Whites for this appalling state of affairs the Negro, it explains, is a victim of race discrimination; he does not have the same job opportunities; he finds it harder to come by a regular income; his family life falls to pieces; and so he is more liable to get into trouble, etc.

Confusion is added to confusion by learned studies from the universities all based on the totally erroneous assumption that all races are exactly the same except for superficial differences like colour, and that whatever differences appear later must all be traced to differences of environment.

All this ingenious theorising can be knocked on the head with one simple question which anyone calling himself a sociologist or psychologist should be able to answer: How do the Negroes live along the West Coast of Africa, whence most of America's Negroes came originally as slaves? What does the Negro "family" look like in that part of the world where he can hardly be said to be a victim of racial discrimination?

The answer, of course, is that in West Africa, as among the pure and relatively pure Negroes all over the African continent, the family as known in Europe, America and Asia is seldom to be found. In Nigeria and Ghana, in particular, where the primeval tribal system has broken down under the impact of the White man's civilisation, most families consist of mother and children, with a "husband" or "father" fulfilling only a transient role.

The matriarchal system is as old as Africa — which helps to explain why in this part of the world most private property and most small businesses are in the hands of the women, typical of whom are the famous "Mammy traders" of Lagos and Accra.

The only exceptions to this rule are the men made rich by Western-style politics — like the politician who ordered a golden bed — and members of certain racial minorities like the Hausa who have a strong ingredient of non-negroid blood in their veins.

All this is quite easily explained. Among the pure Negroes the important unit is the tribe; and it is to the tribe and not the man who fathers her children that the woman looks for protection and status.

Race studies are falsified today and the truth suppressed for the same reason that other sciences, especially astronomy, were falsified in the Middle Ages — because the truth threatens the prevailing political power structure and its long-range aims.

Academicians who promote the liberal line know that an honest recognition of inherent differences of race, giving rise to unalterable differences of life-style, are a barrier to those forces which are today working for the centralisation of all political power in a single world government. These academicians depend on these same forces for success and public acclaim in their careers.

Obviously, if races are different they will need for their maximum fulfilment and happiness local government which they themselves can influence and control.

As we have said before in this service, the Negro in the United States is being crucified as a race by those who pretend to be his friends and defenders but are intersted in him only to the extent that they can use him, cruelly exploiting for politcal purposes the agony and anger resulting from his failure to make the White man's life-style his own.

PROBLEMS ARE SOLVED

All over the world human nature fights back as strenuous efforts are made to promote policies which deny deep-rooted differences of racial life-style and aptitude. In a word, nowhere can the so-called multi-racial "deal" be made to work.

A sample, taken at random, of the incessant race-mixing propaganda pumped out by the newspapers of the South African liberal establishment:

> LUSAKA: The happy sound of children's laughter drifted over the fence . . . about 20 youngsters in the nursery were playing . . . Their faces, White, Brown and Black, were alive with happiness.
>
> There was laughter, too, later that same evening in the roadside bar crowded with Black faces. Not one White person was to be seen.
>
> And there was laughter in the club on the other side of town where rich English county accents vied with thick Afrikaans voices for attention from the Black barmen.
>
> The failure of Zambia's seven-year-old multi-racial society to bridge the colour gap is still today one of the most insoluble problems facing this young nation. *(Daily News).*

The obvious question: Whose "problem" is it? The Blacks who are laughing so happily in their pub do not seem to be aware of any unsolved problem; nor are the laughing Whites in their club.

So, whose is the "problem" of bridging a colour gap which people of different colour themselves do not wish to bridge?

It is the problem of a tiny minority of hidden power-wielders who regard the needs and wishes of ordinary people as obstacles that must somehow be circumvented or removed.

Examples are provided daily in the newspapers. "American Voters Cry off Social Experiment", cries *The Daily News* (Durban) over a report which tells us: "The racial integration of American schools is reaching the end of the line. The voters have at last had enough of the huge social experiment — and the social upheaval — that began with the famous 1954 Supreme Court decision outlawing segregated school systems".

Not satisfied with virtually altering the United States Constitution by interpreting it as it was obviously never meant to be interpreted, the courts went on to insist that races must be mixed in the schools even at the cost of transporting children many miles so as to achieve the requisite racial balance.

The result was that bus-loads of children from the Black slums were poured into the White neighbourhood schools and bus-loads of White children poured into the schools in the Black slumlands.

Whose was the "problem" the American courts were trying to "solve"? Most certainly not that of the parents of the children, as we now learn.

Those who are not wilfully blind — that is, those who do not have some personal vested interest in the suppression of the truth, will find on all sides proof that South Africa's traditional policy of race separation is sound and correct, and that the enforced mixing of people of widely divergent races and cultures produces the worst possible results for all concerned.

Part of the proof will be found in those places which have been protected from the evil of enforced race-mixing— Iceland, for example.

The *Washington Observer* tells us that when more than 4,000 U.S. servicemen were stationed in one of America's biggest overseas military bases, in Iceland, there were "no muggings or rapes" in Keflavik, nor were there any such incidents in nearby Keykjavik, where the servicemen went on their short leave. The drug problem in that privileged area was also negligible, as against U.S. Government estimates that 75% of U.S. servicemen in Saigon, Vietnam, take drugs and likewise nearly as many in Germany.

The explanation is simple, says the *Washington Observer:* "The secret of the absence of muggings, rapes and dope-pushing achieved in Keflavik was simply that the U.S. military command there was instructed, as its first order of priority, to see that there would be no Negroes within their jurisdiction, and were given the necessary authority to decide who was or was not coming to Iceland for his tour of duty".

The reason of state behind those instructions was that the then pro-American, right-wing Government of Iceland

had made it an express condition for allowing U.S. bases
in that country.

Says the *Washington Observer:* "The moral of the story
is that the U.S. Defence Department knows only too well
how to cope with narcotics and crime in the armed services
when it has to".

DISSECTING A RACIAL MYSTIQUE

*No one must lightly dismiss the question of race.
It is the key to world history and it is precisely
for this reason that written history so often lacks
clarity—it is written by people who do not understand the race question and what belongs to it.
Language and religion do not make a race, only
blood does that. — Benjamin Disraeli.*

A subject which has been made topical in a number
of learned journals in the United States, following the
publication of Professor Ernest van der Haag's *The Jewish
Mystique,* is the claimed superiority of the Jewish intellectual
apparatus" as a possible explanation of the truly astonishing
predominance in wealth, power and influence of a tiny
Jewish minority in the Western world.

We may be sure there is some truth in the claim put
forward by Dr. Nathaniel Weyl *(The Creative Elite in
America)* and others that centuries of "selection for intelligence" has played an important part in the evolution of a
Jewish race and nation with an exceptionally high average
standard of intelligence and a truly remarkable dearth of
fools and misfits.

We also know that the same "intellectual apparatus"
works differently in different circumstances and in response
to different stimuli, and we know, or ought to know, that the
peculiar circumstances of the Jewish people, always a tiny
minority in a human environment which they feel to be
potentially hostile, must have the effect of prodding their
minds into alertness and activity.

What we really want to find out is whether the present
extraordinary disparity is the product only of a superior
"intellectual apparatus" or whether there are other important
factors involved.

How, for example, are we to reconcile the present
apparent disparity in performance with the indisputable
fact that the whole might of the West, the civilisation which

has today spread its influence all over the globe, is essentially a product of the energy and creative genius of the Western European people?

How do we reconcile the present competitive inadequacy of the Western European with a recognition of the mighty powers of mind and spirit whose achievements in every field of human endeavour, especially in architecture, art, music and literature, represents to this day, after centuries of competitive striving, the highwater mark of human achievement?

We cannot hope to be able to understand the world in which we live and our own situation in that world if we are unable or afraid to try to find the answers to questions like these.

We know also that there have been lengthy periods in history when the inferior status of the Jewish people has contrasted markedly with the power, confidence and brilliant achievement of the people among whom they dwelt; and we are not aware that such inferior status was ever attributed to any *inferiority* of the Jewish intellectual appratus".

One part of the explanation of the apparent contradiction, we believe, can be traced to the well-established fact that the human mind can function in radically different ways. It can function solely at the service of the individual, when it fully deserves the description of an "apparatus". Or it can function almost entirely at the service of the community, when it is not so much an apparatus as a super-personal phenomenon, a sort of cyclonic funnel drawing to its centre and expressing in works the entire cultural resources of the race.

Western achievement has never depended on a high average of intellectual activity but more often on the exceptional performance of a few gifted individuals. Those who form the bulk of the population are then naturally inclined to coast along as comfortably as possible, sharing and enjoying the benefits provided by the activated few, propping up and carrying along with them many who might otherwise fail to keep up, and carrying along with them also a genetic inheritance capable of throwing up more exceptional individuals when these are required.

This phenomenon of the exceptional individual is better known as genius, where the great tidal flow of race energy and will forces itself impetuously and turbulently through the narrow strait of the individual mind, too often at terrible cost to the individual concerned.

Only by an unusual accident of circumstances has the Western European brand of originating and pioneering excellence any chance of exhibiting itself today, one example of this being space travel, which calls for rare qualities of character as well as a good "intellectual apparatus". This may explain the resentful and vindictive condemnation of the Moon Project by writers, like Norman Mailer, and newspapers of America's money establishment like the *Washington Post*.

What it all comes to is that prevailing historic circumstances, including the almost complete domination of the economic motive in modern life, are as advantageous to the Jewish people as they are disadvantageous to the Western European people, depriving them almost entirely of outlets for the kind of mental activity which has always been the secret of their greatness.

The disparity continues to widen as private-ownership capitalism degenerates at an accelerating pace into anonymous finance-capitalism.

The "degeneration" refers, of course, to the fact that the displacement of private-ownership capitalism is one of the evil results of the betrayal by governments of one of their most important social responsibilites — that of preventing the emergence of concentrations of economic power large enough and strong enough to control government itself, all this being part of the process whereby the Western European, whether in Europe or elsewhere, has been largely dispossessed of the control of his own destiny.

For this state of affairs the Western European has no one to blame except himself, because in making money and material possession the only measure of value, he created an environment and a complex of human relationships more advantageous to the energetic and self reliant Jewish minority than to people of his own kind.

The results we see all around us. The essential Western European, whether he be an Englishman, a Frenchman, a German, an American or a South African, is afflicted with a form of soul-sickness which undermines his morale, stifles imagination and enterprise and inhibits mental activity in all its forms, an illness which naturally varies in intensity according to personal circumstances.

Unable to be true to himself, the Western European has become the victim of cultural and political distortion, the main symptoms as experienced by the individual being the lack of a sense of direction and purpose; in other words, a haunting sense of the futility of existence, all concentrated finally in an intense desire, most keenly felt by young people, to kick over and destroy the prevailing order.

It is not enough, however, to say that the Western European is today afflicted with soul-sickness and to make an inventory of these symptoms and consequences of that sickness.

What we need, if we are to do ourselves any good, is to gain an insight into the etiology of it, tracing with precision the nature of the distortion and the causes which lie immediately behind the symptoms. And that means, before all else, knowing something about the political nature of man. After all, how can we hope to be able to identify and understand a distortion of moral and political identity if we do not already possess in our minds a reasonably clear picture of the pattern before it was distorted.

The entire known history of the human race will confirm that man is essentially a social animal and that he needs, as one of the first requirements of his moral health, the security provided by a sense of community or sense of belonging, which is something he has never been able to find hitherto except in some circumscribed group or community made up of individuals much the same as himself.

Inseparable from such a pattern of existence which has persisted through millennia and is shared by the greater part of the animal kingdom, is a dual code of attitude and conduct clearly designed by nature to preserve that pattern —inside the group, amity and co-operation and mutual sympathy (even if spiced with a little competition between the individuals composing it); towards all those outside the group, an attitude of indifference which can harden into hostility and conflict, as circumstances dictate.

The individual living in such an environment is never morally confused. "These people," he says to himself, in effect, "are my people. These I can trust and they can trust me. I help them and they help me." He draws a deep-rooted sense of security from the knowledge that there are people joined to him by a shared set of interests and obligations. Operating from such a firm base of security, he is prepared to risk his life, nay, even willingly sacrifice it, giving his all to the group from which he derives all.

What the individual then calls his "conscience" is part of the psychological machinery required to ensure that he always maintains towards other individuals in the group, or towards the group as a whole, a code of attitude and conduct calculated to serve the best interests of the group and of all the individuals composing that group.

The moral and political distortion which afflicts the people of Western European origin can thus be ascribed to the obliteration of the ancient boundaries separating groups of self-consciously similar people and their absorption and intermingling in larger politcal units.

The individual, saddled with a psychology which is the evolutionary product of millennia of experience, now finds himself on the horns of a dilemma. Drawn or forced into a heterogeneous human environment, he brings with him, and cannot be parted from, a deep-rooted need for a *homogeneous* human environment. The psychology of the dual code has been built into the cells of his body and brain.

But how, in a heterogeneous society with its strange new matrix of relationships dictated by an economic ordering of society, does he distinguish between "us" and "them", between those who belong with him and those who don't? Even more painful is his dilemma when he finds himself in a greatly expanded political unit which includes people widely different in race and life style, in some cases not even sharing with him the same language?

The result for the Western European individual is inner conflict and confusion. His responses, instead of being simple and clear-cut, as they would be in the simpler form of society whence he emerged, are mixed up in such a way as to produce psychological disturbances, including guilt feelings and a weakened morale. The individual is divided within himself and his creative and intellectual potential greatly reduced, likewise his capacity for effective combination with other individuals of his own kind.

The trouble does not end there — far from it! Society itself shows signs of deep inner division as the many soul-sick individuals tend to cluster together according to the way in which they seek individually to resolve their dilemma of a dual code which has ceased to work, giving rise eventually to two major groupings which we can identify with the terms *Right* and *Left.*

On the Right are those who hope to find salvation in the re-establishment of smaller, more homogeneous units of humanity in which the psychology of the dual code can once again be made to work freely; or, at any rate, resist all those influences tending towards the creation of still larger, more heterogeneous political units, culminating even in the possibility of a one-world state.

Conspicuous among those on the Left are individuals in whom intellect has been developed at the expense of instinct, and who now seek salvation in an imagined world in which all people will be equal and undifferentiated and in which mankind's primordial heritage of a dual code can be replaced with a single code of universal amity and brotherhood.

Thus a conflict which originates inside the individual is transferred to society itself, even dividing families, and creating a situation which any alien minority can exploit to its own advantage.

We cannot know all this is going to work out in the years ahead, but we do know for sure that the psychological disturbances which arise out of efforts to apply a single code of universal amity and equality in a two-code world which no one can change, constitutes a form of soul-sickness which has everywhere reduced the moral and political potential of the Western European people, and has created conditions highly advantageous to a small Jewish minority which has never allowed itself to be separated from its ancient two-code psychology.

The key to this unique minority advantage is a system of institutionalised learning, reinforced by religion, which makes it possible for the Jewish people to preserve an intensely self-conscious racial and national unity *in dispersion,* whereas for others national and racial unity has always depended on geographical boundaries. Instead, Jewish race-consciousness and nationalism have become all the more intense for having been confined entirely to the mind.

The science of anthropology has had to be falsified and smothered to a truly astonishing degree to prevent information of this kind being universally known and understood. As we have pointed out before, many of those sciences whose purpose it is to help man to understand himself — anthropology, psychology, genetics — are in the same state of eclipse today as were astronomy and other sciences in the Middle Ages, and for the same reason: that their findings threaten the foundations of existing power structures, whether these be religious or political or financial.

It may, therefore, come as a surprise to some of our readers to learn that what is written above has long been known by scientists and thinkers who have managed to remain loyal to the highest ideals of Western intellectual courage and honesty.

Whole volumes could be quoted, of which the following, from the writings of the late Sir Arthur Keith, world-famous anthropologist and former President of the British Association for the Advancement of Science, is only a tiny sample, and must here suffice:

> Another mark of race possessed by the Jews must be mentioned. Their conduct is regulated by a 'dual code'; their conduct towards their felows is based on one code (amity), and that towards all who are outside their circle on another (enmity). The use of the dual code, as we have seen, is a mark of an evolving race. My deliberate opinion is that racial characters are more strongly developed in the Jews than in any other Caucasian people.
>
> My anthropological colleagues, under the spell of ethical ideals, have done Gentiles and Jews an ill-service by giving euphonious names to vulgar things. They have assured the Jews that they are not a race but only an 'ethnic group' kept together by having a religion in common. They also have assured all the other Caucasian peoples that they are raceless, and that hence all the animosity which arises between Gentile and Jew is an artificially fomented form of hysteria. With the best intentions in the world, professional anthropologists have succeeded in hiding from the world the nature of its running sores. If these sores are to be cured, they must be exposed freely to the surgeon's scrutiny, and have their proper names given to them. (*A New Theory of Human Evolution*, pages 390-1.)

Politcal commentators and analysts who decline for one reason or another to probe below the surface for causes of what is happening in the world today, so far from making any contribution to public enlightenment, and are only helping to thicken the fog of confusion in which millions of the soul-sick flounder.

We have said it before, and we say it again: A strong sense of group identity, pride of race, nationalism — call it what you will — gives people a strong sense of purpose and direction which renders them almost totally immune to the culturally and morally subversive influences which are rampant in the Western world, all utterly destructive of the health and happiness of mankind.

We have a marvellous opportunity in Southern Africa of infusing a rich national spirit in our young people. Our whole history and Christian civilisation point the way.

THE NEW SCRAMBLE FOR AFRICA

ADDRESSING a private and confidential dinner party arranged by the leftist Rhodesian Constitutional Association in Salisbury, October 1, 1965, the United States Consul-General, Mr. Roswell D. McClelland made a statement which contains the key to a question which has continued to baffle many Rhodesians and South Africans:.

Why is it that the Free World, which is supposed to be fighting Communism, is so hostile to anti-Communist Rhodesia and South Africa?

The question could be put differently: Why are those who are supposed to be locked in a struggle with world Communism always in the forefront of the anti-anti-Communists?

The American Consul-General said this: "Africa today is in the throes of revolutionary change; and there is as much legitimacy in revolution as there is in government."

A copy of McClelland's typewritten speech, with alterations and corrections in his own handwriting, came into the possession of the Rhodesian Government at the time when the present writer was employed by the Government as Information Adviser.

Needless to say, McClelland was not talking about the unilateral declaration of independence which was then little more than a month away, for he went on to say: "Indeed, an African leader has to be a revolutionary if he is to remain in power. To be otherwise is to defend the status quo; and the status quo was colonialism."

What the American representative was telling the Rhodesian Constitutional Association was that the United States was no less on the side of revolution in Africa than the Soviet Union or Communist China.

This explains in a few words why the United States and the Communist countries have always been in step in demanding and working for the overthrow of the present regime in Rhodesia and why they continue to express much the same attitude towards South Africa and the Portuguese provinces in Africa.

McClelland made it clear in his Salisbury address that the United States and the Communist States are not partners In promtoing revolution in Africa — far from it! They are rivals! Or so he believes.

What he said, in effect, was this: If you don't let us manage the revolution the Communists will and that will be much worse for you.

His exact words: "It is the innate role of the revolutionary, and this applies *a fortiori* to the still White-dominated southern part of the continent, to change an existing and unsatisfactory order."

The question arises: Why is America, the leader of the Free World, helping to promote this revolution in Africa? We have the American Consul-General's reply: "Not to do so would be an intolerable betrayal of the moral and politcal principles which are not only an integral part of the fabric of American life but have provided the main impulsion for human progress in the 20th Century: democracy, self-determination, human rights and racial equality."

The United States thus claims to be helping to promote revolution in Africa for moral and altruistic reasons.

With the Communist bloc, of course, it is different—"The Communist role has been rather to seize upon the highly-charged and ready-made issue of liberation and to exacerbate and exploit it to Communism's own needs, not necessarily those of the Africans"—McClelland's own words.

No one needs to be reminded that they are helping to promote revolution in Africa; each one claims to be doing it for purely altruistic reasons; each accuses the other of doing it for purposes that have to do with the expansion of power and influence.

We may be sure that precisely the same formula applies In South-East Asia, especially in Vietnam, where the Americans have had armed forces more than twice as numerous as the White population of Rhodesia.

A global power struggle which in the last century took the form of nation against nation, today takes the form of a conflict between two giant power blocs or combinations the Western, dominated by the United States, and the Communist, still dominated by the Soviet Union.

If it were as simple as that, how simple it would be! But if we cannot see it, we begin at any rate to sniff the presence of some third force. We begin to realise as we assemble and try to put together the known facts that, as Dr. Bella Dodd, former member of the National Committee of the U.S. Communist Party, put it, "the Communist conspiracy is merely part of a much bigger conspiracy." This can only mean that there are powerful occult forces which have a foot in both camps, making sure that a "Free world" which does nearly all the paying will always be the loser in the revolutionary race.

As Douglas Reed pointed out in *Somewhere South of Suez*, President Truman's "Point 4 Plan," announced in 1949, bore the closest possible resemblance to a plan for Africa set out some years earlier by Earl Browder, then leader of the United States Communist Party, in his book, *Teheran, Our Path in War and Peace*.

"Only those near to President Truman can know who persuaded him of the merits of the idea," wrote Reed. "It is obvious, however, where the idea came from in the first place. Once more the paramount fact of our time is established: the actual aims of American high policy and of the Communist empire are not separate or opposite but the same. There must be in America, under President Truman as under President Roosevelt, some group of force strong or persuasive enough to 'sell' Communist aims to political leaders, and simultaneously convince them that these will 'stop Communism'. Here is a Communist idea presented to the American Congress and people as one of several ways of thwarting Communist expansion. It is, in fact, exactly what the Communist empire wants for its own long-sighted ends."

Dr. Franco Nogueira, Portugal's former Foreign Minister, has described what has been happening since Mr. Harold Macmillan's "Winds of Change" began to blow in 1960:

"Africa has been subjected to a regime that excludes European interests and African interests as well, neither being sufficiently strong to impose themselves. Each of the two blocs has made a supreme ideological principle out of the political actions and of the strategic roles which are most likely to bring about the defeat of the adversary."

This explains why neither of the two major power blocs which are promoting revolution in Africa is interested in setting up genuinely independent states on this continent.

For each requires states which can be handled like dough and kneaded into the greater lump of its existing sphere of influence.

This is how Dr. Nogueira puts it: "A form of autonomy and independence has been created which ensures the destruction of the old forms of sovereignty and permits the setting up of new forms of sovereignty so precarious and so artificial that it is an easy matter to dominate them. A method has been adopted that leads to the transfer of political power unaccompanied by a transfer of the other forms of power (economic, cultural and military) which, in fact, determine policy. The result is that the real authority and the real control are to be found outside the frontiers of the new political units."

So now we know, or ought to know, why Katanga's independence had to be overthrown at any cost. Katangan independence would have been the genuine article because copper-rich Katanga possessed those "other forms of power" which would have rendered her self-sufficient and incapable of being manipulated from abroad.

Portugal's rulers have got the picture quite clear: "That is why each of the great power blocs seeks to get hold of the control of these new countries and for this purpose, notwithstanding their antagonism, they take the same steps— aid to terroist and revolutionary organisations, international condemnation of titular sovereign powers and the weakening of them, erosion of public opinion in the metropolitan country and overseas, financial, technical and military aid to the new political units, drawing them into systems of alliance, economic blocs and spheres of influence which gradually deprive them of any really independent action or the means to take it. These are the outlines of what is today conventionally termed anti-colonialism."

"This ruthless political action," added the Portuguese Foreign Minister, "is shielded by high ideological aims."

Both power blocs promote the myth that the principle of one-man-one-vote ensures respect for human rights, guarantees individual liberty, encourages economic development and thus provides the right conditions for politcal stability.

The question might well be asked why the two power blocs continue to promote and exploit his myth when it has been demonstrated time and time again that where implemented it produces results almost exactly the opposite of those sought.

The truth emerges with ever-increasing clarity; because the main result of the implementation of one-man-one-vote is precisely that which is required by both power blocs–"the destruction of the old forms" and the making way for "new forms, so precarious and so artificial that it is an easy matter to dominate them."

So we see that the two power blocs, one centred in Washington and the other in Moscow, have precisely the same primary requirements as they promote the revolution in Africa.

Again, with that Third Force making sure that the West foots all the bills but does not win!

The same key unlocks mysteries in other parts of the world.

In Cuba both the Americans and the Russians were supporting Fidel Castro's revolution against a Batista regime which neither could manipulate and which — believe it or not — had actually severed diplomatic relations with the Soviet Union.

All over Latin America the same pattern has been repeated again and again — no government is tolerated that is genuinely indigenous and independent and cannot be controlled from without.

Washington and Moscow both support any revolutionary movements aimed at a government which they would both describe as "reactionary" — in other words, a government which insists on being master in its own house.

Really effective anti-Communists like Wesson y Wesson in Santo Domingo and the Diems, who were winning in Vietnam with very little help from the Americans, were undermined and replaced with leaders who were more acceptable to leftist forces in the United States.

Is it any wonder that the West continues to lose ground in its struggle against Communism? How can it ever hope to win? For who can hold his own with the devil in a contest in which both make mischief with fire? Who can hope to be able to beat the Communists at the revolutionary game?

What it comes to is that the West tries to fight Communism with leftism; they fight a leftism that is red-hot with another leftism which is luke-warm, at the same time making it only too easy for hardened Communist agents to infiltrate their own ranks, as did Alger Hiss (one of Roosevelt's principal aides at Yalta) and Owen Lattimore (who played so important a part in handing over China to that "great agrarian reformer", Mao tse Tung).

We have much to learn from the Portuguese in this kind of struggle.

First question: How have the Portuguese managed to hold out after all the other colonial powers have been driven out of Africa?

Reply: In Portugal politics has remained in power and has not become subordinate to economics. True enough, the Portuguese have not shared the runaway industrial and and commercial development so much in evidence in the other Western states. But they have not made the Gross National Product their god. Therefore, in Portugal economics is the servant, not the master. The Portuguese understand that in the life of man there are considerations more important than the purely material ones.

"We are often asked," said Dr. Nogueira "whether we are not being too rigid and inflexible in refusing to listen to others. Would it not be better to try to soothe away the hate of others by yielding a little in what is secondary, the better to save what is fundamental? Should we not try to gain support of some great Powers by trying to satisfy them in theory, by some declaration of intention even if in our hearts we do not mean to carry it out in practice?"

How much happier and safer South Africans and Rhodesians would feel if their leaders replied to such questions as the Portuguese have done! Again we quote from Dr. Franco Noguieira:

> "Our adversaries know that if they make the slightest breach in any of our principles, we should at once be at their mercy; we should then be fighting on our critics' ground, not on our own; we should be abandoning the logic of our position to submit to the enemy's logic; without our enemy having accepted anything of our aims we should have accepted everything that others want to thrust on us. There can be no partial compliance, no possible stop half-way down the slope. We must realise once and for all that the enemy's aim is not to bring into Angola or Mozambique human rights, individual liberty and collective progress,

so that all we have to do is to discuss methods that would lead to such ends. No — the aim is to dominate Angola and Mozambique and to include them in the spheres of foreign influences, to utilise their economic and strategic positions for the benefit of other Powers."

What we have in Africa today is only a partial fulfilment of a plan first enunciated by Earl Browder, the Communist leader, and later presented to Congress by President Truman as a statement of American policy.

How many innocent people have been done to death in Africa in the process of trying to realise what President Truman described as "a new type of benevolent imperialism", we shall never know, but we do know for certain that the figure must run into several millions.

We also know that nowhere on the African continent can any Black nation be said to have been liberated and made truly independent.

There does not exist in Africa, nor has there existed, power of the kind needed to bring about the changes we have seen since 1960. The power which has been at work in Africa has always come from outside Africa. The politics of Africa have been revolutionised from outside, not from within.

What that means is that the so-called 'new nations' are not real nations but are the creations of forces centred outside Africa and are like so many pieces on the checkerboard of modern power politics.

When in the long history of the human race have there been real nations totally unable to stand on their own feet, unable to feed themselves or defend themselves? The new states would collapse without handouts and assistance from the West.

What we have had in Africa since 1960 is not a 'liberation' of former colonies but a neo-colonialism, a new scramble for possession conducted in changed circumstances according to a different set of rules. Last century and early in this, it was a scramble in which the competitors were the nations of Europe . . . Now there are only two contenders for possession, two competitors in the 'new scramble for Africa,' two imperialisms — that of the Western liberal establishment, now centred in the United States, and that of the Communist world. Or so it seems!

But behind all the seeming, it is a Janus-headed, one-world, twentieth-century imperialism of money with two faces or aspects.

The so-called nations of Africa which today figure so prominently in the news are mere creations of modern political make-believe. The Black politicians who strut upon the stage of world affairs and attend grandiose conferences in Addis Ababa or Lusaka or Accra, or who attend Commonwealth Prime Ministers' conferences, are mere puppets. Their bombastic speeches and official statements are everywhere accepted, widely publicised and gravely analysed and commented on in the news media of the whole world. The truth is that, almost without exception, these speeches and statements have been written by so-called White 'advisers', who are, in fact, the agents of those powers behind the scenes which have revolutionised the continent of Africa and are trying to revolutionise the whole world.

Thus, what looks like power in the new African states is not real power — it is a derived power from sources outside Africa. In a word, Black nationalism is a White hand in a Black glove.

Those who know and understand how and by whom the revolutionary changes of the last ten years have been brought about in Africa, and for what reasons, are not puzzled by the weird contradictions and inconsistencies which appear upon the surface.

THE EXAMPLE OF ZAMBIA

Zambia provides as good an example as any of the Alice-in-Wonderland atmosphere of unreality that prevails in a country where Communism and super-capitalism seem to have settled down to live happily ever after.

Since independence there has been a systematic elimination of all traces of the former ties with colonialist Britain — well, not quite all. British expatriate workers and technical advisers have been replaced with people from behind the Iron and Bamboo curtains. Among the first to go, and that in rather undignified circumstances, were the British air force and army personnel.

Quite unperturbed by a succession of slaps in the face, the British Government continues to pour millions of pounds in foreign aid into Zambia, while the Americans continue to talk and act as if this is one part of Africa where their policy of "benevolent imperialism" is paying off.

The huge copper mining industry is nationalised with a stroke of the pen, and Harry Oppenheimer, multi-millionaire head of one of the owning groups tells shareholders that the decision was to be welcomed and that Anglo-American had been "hoping that the Government would participate as a shareholder."

The Zambian Government did not even have to find the money for its 51 per cent share — this, said an official announcement, would be paid for out of future earnings!

We may be sure that all this is not half as crazy as it seems and that it makes good sense to those who, in the words of Dr. Murray Butler, "make things happen." They evidently have good reasons for not telling us what they are doing.

If our democracy is not too degenerate into a world-wide totalitarianism that will blight the lives of our children and their children, it is important that as many of us as possible should penetrate the barrier of secrecy and join that "somewhat larger group" who understand what they see happening.

Not surprisingly, the report of the Zambian Government's "purchase" or shares in the copper mining industry was accompanied by an official announcement that "there will be a wage freeze in the mining industry and unofficial strikes will be banned".

Since President Kaunda's United National Independence Party also controls the labour unions, we may be sure there will be no strikes at all, and that the process of Zambianisation, or replacement of White labour with Black, will not be permitted to increase working costs.

Directors nominated by the Zambian Government will nominally control the separate mining companies while the holding companies, both foreign dominated, remain untouched. At the mining company level, however, the influence of the Zambian directors must be minimal, since most decisions are left to the general manager and are of a technical nature seldom requiring more than formal approval by the board of directors.

The really important power continues to be wielded by Anglo American and Roan Selection Trust, both linked with still bigger industrial giants abroad which dominate the world's copper market.

Politics is a game in which seeing is not always believing. It seems as if Dr. Kaunda is now more powerful than before. What has happened is that Dr. Kaunda and the UNIP hierarchy have been manoeuvred into a position where they can be more easily controlled and manipulated from abroad, and the "independence" of their country under "creeping socialism" more plainly revealed.

Innumerable other signs combine to suggest that the nationalisation of Zambian copper is part of an overall plan to establish Zambia a powerful base for possible Vietnam-style operations against Rhodesia, the Portuguese provinces, and the Republic of South Africa.

Can it be by pure chance that all these moves which Western super-capitalism promotes or approves are so highly advantageous to the Communists?

Both required the suppression of Biafran independence. The United Kingdom paid most of the cost of this operation and supplied the war material used by the Federal forces. The Soviet Union supplied the aircraft, piloted by Czechs, along with the necessary ground staff.

Both also required the suppression of Katangan independence in 1961, the only difference being that the Soviet Union flatly refused to contribute one cent to the cost of the United Nations operation.

Reports which are published from time to time of British and American reaction to the expansion of Soviet and Communist Chinese power in the Indian Ocean area can only have the effect of increasing bewilderment in the public mind. If the nations of the West are worried over what is hapepning in that strategically important area, then why do they not suit their actions to their words and do something about it? Why do they consistently behave as if they could not care less?

For the last three years South Africa has been pressing the United Kingdom to resume the supply of maritime arms for the defence of the Cape sea route, now so much more important after the closing of the Suez Canal.

The South African Prime Minister, Mr. John Vorster, has said on more than one occasion that he is at a loss to understand the attitude of the Western nations in view of the obvious increase in Communist power and influence in the Indian Ocean.

Most puzzling of all for those who know only what they are told by their newspapers is the attitude of the United States which has lost something like 50,000 lives and poured out a vast fortune in Vietnam — all for the purpose, so it is said, of halting Communism expansion in that part of the world!

Let us hope that Mr. Vorster was only expressing himself rhetorically when he said he was "at a loss to understand" all this. No national leader has any excuse for not understanding the massive campaign of propaganda and pressure aimed at South Africa after the lesson of what happened to anti-Communist China and anti-Communist Cuba, and more recently to anti-Communist Greece.

RHODESIA — POLICY OF RETREAT

It is perfectly clear now that Mr. Ian Smith did not know what he was doing when on November 11, 1965, the Rhodesian Government issued its famous Unilateral Declaration of Independence.

First big surprise for Mr. Smith was the dazzling display of propaganda fireworks which greeted the announcement that Rhodesia had decided to give formal effect to a *de facto* state of self-government which had continued uninterrupted since 1923.

He could not have been more surprised if he had accidentally touched a bare high-tension power cable with the point of a screwdriver.

Mr. Smith found himself almost overnight a world celebrity. While the Liberal Establishment with its media of mass communication reviled him, it was equally obvious that conservatives everywhere, deeply stirred by some of Mr. Smith's public utterances, greeted him as a hero, as the first important political leader this century who had had the courage to say to the Liberalist-Communist conspirators: "So far and no further!"

The reaction of a world-famous writer like Douglas Reed was symptomatic of what was happening everywhere after November 11th, 1965 — Mr. Reed ended a literary silence which had lasted more than 15 years; he came to Rhodesia and wrote another best-seller, *The Battle for Rhodesia.*

The only possible explanation of what has hapepned since November, 1965, is that Mr. Smith was convinced that the U.D.I. would be a nine-day wonder, that the British Government would quickly come to its senses and the Rhodesians left alone, as in the past, to manage their own affairs.

How else are we to explain the timing of the U.D.I. and Rhodesia's state of almost complete unpreparedness for everything that was to follow?

Nothing could have been more radical than the challenge of the Unilateral Declaration of Independence.

Nothing could be less radical than the actions and policies of the Rhodesian Government since the British Government picked up the gauntlet.

A loud shout of defiance has been followed by frenzied efforts to pacify and come to terms with the opponent.

From the very beginning, the Smith Government set about disowning and dismantling its own rightwing image, created partly by itself in the succession of election campaigns which placed the Rhodesian Front Party in power and partly by friends all around the world who had been stirred to great enthusiasm by what looked like an event of world-historical importance — one small nation's open defiance of the Liberal-Communist world conspiracy.

And it goes without saying that Rhodesia could not disown its own rightwing image without at the same time brushing off innumerable organisations which had sprung to its defence, and disappointing good friends like Douglas Reed.

Liberty Lobby, one of the most powerful conservative organisations in the United States with headquarters in Washington and a subscriber list running into a quarter of a million, including many journalists, radio and television commentators and other opinion formers, spent 40,000 dollars on a single operation publicising the Rhodesian Government's own reply to the accusations of the leftists. This campaign included full-page advertisements in newspapers with nation-wide circulations. Yet the only acknowledgement from the Rhodesian Government was a cyclostyled letter bearing the signature of the Prime Minister's private secretary.

Members of the British parliamentary group known as

the Monday Club were shocked at the cool treatment they received in Salisbury—"brush-off" expresses more accurately the treatment they received. Meanwhile (and in spite of the kind of treatment) it was left to members of the Monday Club to continue to harass the British Prime Minister, Mr. Harold Wilson, in the House of Commons.

What can all this mean except that having acted radically in making a unilateral declaration of independence, there was totally lacking in Mr. Smith and the Rhodesian Front hierarchy any will to go on acting radically?

Perfect conditions were thus created for the massive penetration of the ranks of the Rhodesian Front by members of the former opposition United Party, with the result that in a few years Mr. Ian Smith has transformed the Rhodesian Front into an almost perfect replica of the party it defeated so overwhelmingly at the polls in 1962.

"If Rhodesia falls, the move for war against South Africa will immediately gain momentum in New York . . ."
—Douglas Reed.

MIDDLE EAST JIGSAW PUZZLE

A country which can utterly destroy all its neighbours in six days can hardly be said to be insecure. It is difficult to think of any other country in the world which is so secure — Glubb Pasha, The Middle East Crisis.

THE ordinary newspaper reader's reaction to news from the Middle East can only be described as one of almost total bewilderment.

In a confused sort of way he understands, or thinks he understands, that the Israelis are the "good guys" and the Arabs the "bad guys", that Israel is on the side of the West while the Arab states are on the side of the Soviet Communists.

The confused picture of the Middle East situation which we have been getting for 20 years and more from the mass media of communication has only one possible explanation — the Middle East represents an area of maximum falsification of news and suppression of genuine public debate.

Indeed, there are reasons for all the falsification and suppression — if the average American or Briton understood events in the Middle East he would automatically know a great deal more than his masters consider good for him; he would know, for example, what are the influences at work in his own country; he would know how the machinery of party politics can be manipulated and political leaders put under irresistible pressure to promote policies totally at variance with the interests of the people they are supposed to serve.

Meanwhile, the state of public bewilderment serves our "new unhappy lords" very well, since purposes are being pursued on a worldwide scale which simply do not bear honest examination and discussion. In short, a confused public is Requirement No. 1; better still, a public which has abandoned all attempts to understand what is going on and allows its attention to be occupied exclusively with a multitude of issues which have no bearing whatever on major developments threatening its future existence.

With our attention focussed mainly on the Israelis and the Egyptians, we lose sight of the vastly important fact that Soviet Russia has been permitted to replace the Western powers in the eastern Mediterranean.

The policy of the Western Powers in the Middle East has been dictated not by the real interests of those powers but only by powerful pressures and influences exerted directly on the governments concerned from within, with consequences which could involve all of them in the holocaust of another world war.

All this has been made possible by an almost total embargo on any genuine public discussion of the roles of Zionism and Communism and a suppression of information on a scale unparalleled in history.

The result has been the generation of an impenetrable fog in the realm of public opinion on which is now projected, as on a screen in a darkened room, the popular illusion that by supporting Israel against Egypt we are "opposing" Russian Communism, when all we are really doing is to promote Communist purposes by making it possible for the Soviet Union to establish a powerful bridgehead in an area strategically more important than any other in the world.

Surely the time must come when people will rise in revolt against a tyranny which prohibits any public discussion which does not assume in advance that the Israelis are our friends and are always right and the Arabs are our enemies and always wrong!

The newspapers and other media can hardly be blamed because the tyranny we mention is real and can come down heavily on those who dare to cast any doubt on the authorised version of contemporary history. One newspaper editor or assistant editor frankly admitted as much when asked by a leader of the Muslim Indian community in Durban to print a letter presenting part of the Arab point of view on the Middle East.

"We dare not print it", he said without a blush.

Newspaper owners have too many hostages to fortune, they are too closely integrated with the economic system to be able to play the role of St. George riding against the Dragon of a massive political deceit.

Here, then, are a few basic propositions which call for full information and discussion — and refutation, if possible.

• There is no basic antagonism between the Soviet Union and Israel.
The Soviet Union was one of the first countries to recognise the new state and was the only country supplying the Israelis with arms during the 1948 fighting which resulted in close on a million Arabs being driven into the Negev desert, where they remain to this day.

• The setting up of a Jewish homeland in Palestine has in no way advanced the interests of the United Kingdom or any other Western country — on the contrary it has permitted the Soviet Union to displace them in an area of overwhelming world-strategical importance.

• By no stretch of imagination can Israel be regarded as a Western bastion which the United States and Britain are under some obligation to support in defence of their own national interests.

• The present attitude of Israeli leaders clearly indicates that they know that they have nothing whatever to fear from the Soviety Union; they know that the Soviet Union is only exploiting the Israeli-Arab quarrel in order to establish themselves in the eastern Mediterranean. Hence, in spite of any amount of Western support and assistance Israel could have no future as a state not authorised and permitted by the Soviet Union.

• The Six-Day War was deliberately precipitated by the Russians who informed Nasser that the Israelis were about to attack his ally Syria, fully knowing that the Egyptians were bound to be disastrously defeated, thus rendering them so much more dependent on Russian support. In any case, the Egyptians never attacked the Israelis but only moved up to their own frontier, so placing themselves in reach of the vastly superior Israeli forces, an opportunity which the Israelis seized without a moment's hesitation.

• With the Egyptians themselves militarily impotent and the Soviet Union by no means opposed to the existence of a Jewish state in the Middle East creating tensions which they can exploit, there does not exist today any real threat to Israel's survival as a state.

• Finally, there are good reasons to believe that Jewish

influence in the Soviet Union is every bit as strong as in the United States, possibly even stronger. Hence no world-wide campaign of anti-Communism remotely comparable with the anti-Fascism that preceded the last war.

Present Israeli activity in all the territory captured from the Arabs in the Six-Day War tends to endorse the above propositions. The Israelis are establishing themselves as settlers with all the confidence of people who know they are going to stay. *The Washington Observer* reports:

> The Israelis are now in the first phase of their exploitation. Israeli is preparing to drill for oil in the Gulf of Suez of the Sinai Peninsula . . . Our State Department is weakly protesting but making no effort to stop American industrial firms aiding the Zionist oil operations.

> . . . Israel took over an Egyptian-Italian offshore oil field in the Gulf of Suez near Abu Rudeis and has been working it. The new drilling would be near this same area. Israel is also planning to take over an Egyptian-American offshore oil field called El Morgan, which is also in the Gulf of Suez but closer to the Egyptian mainland. El Morgan is operated by Pan American Oil Corp., a U.S. company . . . Our State Department will make another feeble protest when Pan America's rich oil properties are expropriated by the Zionists but President Nixon will not halt the delivery of U.S. aircraft, guns and material to Israel.

The developments on the Golan heights in the north-east, territory captured from Syria, are said to be typical of the process of colonisation going on in the occupied territories. Reports *The Washington Observer:*

> On the Golan Heights in Syria, where 60,000 Arabs lived, every Arab who did not escape has been annihilated. The Arabs have been replaced by Jewish settlements. Twelve Israeli kibbutzim (co-operative farms) and para-military settlements called 'Nahal' posts now occupy the Golan Heights, and more settlements are in the making. The biggest installation on the Heights is Golan Kibbutz, which has several hundred civilian settlers. It is a collection of concrete block buildings on the site of the destroyed Arab town of Kuneitra . . .

Yehuda Harell, leader of the Golan Kibbutz, says: 'We are going to stay here. You can be sure of that. Israel has plans for 30 more agricultural settlements of 500 people on the Golan Heights' . . .

The ordinary citizen needs to be alerted to the fact that he is being given an untrustworthy account of events in the Middle East and that what happens in this part of the world concerns him as much as anything that could happen in his own country.

One of the most important correctives is Alfred M. Lilienthal's book *There Goes the Middle East* in which this eminent American Jewish expert warns that unless Western policy makers alter their totally pro-Israel stance, the Soviet will continue to make alarming advances in what is strategically the most important area in the world.

What Mr. Lilienthal wrote in 1957 should command even more respect and attention 13 years later when events have had time to prove how right he was. Already the eastern end of the Mediterranan has become a sort of Russian lake with the Soviet Union firmly established in Egypt.

More light was thrown on the Middle East situation in 1967 by Sir John Clubb (Glubb Pasha) in his book *The Middle East Crisis:*

"Everyone who had any military experience in the Middle East", he wrote, "was fully aware that the Egyptian army had not the slightest chance against the Israelis. I estimated the duration of the battle in the Sinai at 48 hours. In fact, I believe it occupied some 60 hours."

Nothing could be more absurd than to suppose that the Soviet Union "backed the wrong horse" in giving support to the Egyptians. Their policy in seeming to support the Arabs, as events have proved, was designed not to help the Arabs but to extend the area of their own power and influence.

"It is now known", writes Eric Butler in *The American Mercury,* "that the 1967 Arab-Israeli conflict was precipitated by false Soviet reports to Nasser that his Syrian partners in the United Arab Republic were about to be attacked by the Israelis."

He adds: "Those who believe that the Soviet is arming the Arabs so that Israel can be destroyed are the victims of a major propaganda hoax."

Does this interpretation of events in the Middle East seem far fetched? It certainly does! So let us consult someone who really ought to know.

The South African Jewish Times, shortly after the Six-Day War, reported a visit by four leading Israeli Communists to Moscow. Here is part of the report:

> Hardly had the Israeli Communists left the Kremlin gates when rumours began to circulate that they had received 'important assurances'.
>
> Yet there is reason to believe that, if not actually an assurance, the Israeli Communists were given to understand that the Kremlin is not committed to support Nasser in his aggressive plans . . .
>
> To a certain extent this gesture was prompted by a desire to show Nasser that the Soviet leaders understand and appreciate the situation in Israel, where the Communist Party is officially represented in Parliament, has its own Press and may criticise if not actually influence Government policy. No such conditions exist in Egypt. Hence the Israeli Communists were treated as real friends and people of importance.
>
> This importance was emphasised by the very warm reception which the Israeli delegates were later given in editorial offices of the *Sovietisch Heimland.* More than that, the Kremlin went even further in preparing the ground and the warm atmosphere for this visit of the Israeli Communists.

By an amusing coincidence *The Jewish Times* article had as one of its headings the line "Behind the News". The other heading read, *USSR Would Never Support Nasser in a War on the Jewish State.* Indeed, this was a glimpse of the truth "behind the news" provided daily by the world's mass media.

This is only a fragment, but it helps to explain the Soviet Union's apparent feebleness as an ally of the Egyptians; it helps to explain why the Israelis dare to undertake enterprises in Egyptian territory which "heighten the danger of precipitating a major war", apparently unafraid of any interference from the Soviet Union; it helps to explain why the Western Press can take the side of the Israelis in their quarrel with the Arab world and at the same time continue to discuss the possibility of "peaceful co-existence" with the Soviet Union.

THE TRUTH LEAKS OUT

We have on more than one occasion described the Middle East conflict, involving the United States and the Soviet Union as well as Israel and the Arab states, as "an area of maximum falsification of news and suppression of genuine public debate."

At last the Western liberal establishment's Middle East propaganda picture shows signs of crumbling and falling apart as the limits of credibility are reached and exceeded.

The Jewish people themselves are finding it increasingly difficult to reconcile an intense nationalism in Israel with Jewry's traditional anti-nationalism everywhere else in the world, and a few more daring individuals, aware of the danger, are raising their voices in warning and are helping to let some light into the Middle East scene.

Here is a sample, from Isaac Deutscher, a leading Jewish intellectual and an acknowledged authority on the Russian Revolution: "In 1948 when Israel was forming itself into a state we witnessed a curious situation in which the Russians and the Americans — the super-antagonists — joined hands. Together they managed to dislodge the British from the Middle East; and together they acted as midwives in the act of birth of Israel". (*The Non-Jewish Jew*, Isaac Deutscher, 1968.)

Deutscher's story of how the Six-Day War was precipitated clears away much of the smog of confusion and supplies facts which tend to support the theory that somewhere behind the scenes there was collusion between the "super-powers".

We are reminded that the Egyptians were encouraged by the Russians to mobilise and to move their forces into an indefensible position against Israeli's southern border. What we did not know was that on May 26, only a few days before the shooting began in 1967, in the dead of night (2.30 a.m.) the Soviet Ambassador woke up Nasser to give him a grave warning that the Egyptian army must not be the first to fire.

"The Soviet curb," says Deutscher, "was heavy, rude and effective." So effective, it turned out, that Nasser did not even take the most elementary precautions against the possibility of an Israeli attack.

Deutscher asks: "Did the Soviet Ambassador in the course of his nocturnal visit tell Nasser that Moscow was sure that the Israelis would not strike first". Certainly, Nasser behaved as if he had been given some such assurance.

Deutscher sums up as follows: "Having excited Arab fears, encouraged them to risky moves, promised to stand by them, and having brought out their own naval units into the Mediterranean to counter the moves of the American Sixth Fleet, the Russians then tied Nasser hand and feet."

What many of us did not know (because we were not told) was that immediately before the Israelis launched their attack the "hot line" between the White House and the Kremlin went into action and the two super-powers agreed to avoid direct intervention.

With large areas of Arab territory occupied by the Israelis, the Arabs then saw the Soviet Union voting in unison with the Americans in the United Nations General Assembly for a cease-fire to which no conditions for a withdrawal of Israeli troops were attached.

In this atmosphere of increased frankness we were not surprised to find in the December 21, 1971 issue of the American magazine *Newsweek* a report of an interview with King Faisal of Saudi Arabia which would have been unthinkable a year or so ago.

Asked about Soviet influence in the Middle East, King Faisal said: "Zionism and Communism are working hand in glove to block any settlement that will restore peace."

He went on to describe Zionism as "the mother of Communism," adding: "It helped to spread Communism around the world. It is now trying to weaken the U.S. and if the plan succeeds they will inherit the world."

Asked how he reconciled this view with the fact that the Russians and Zionists were on opposite sides in the present Middle East conflict, King Faisal replied: "It's all part of a great plot, a grand conspiracy . . . They are only pretending to work against each other in the Middle East. The Zionists are deceiving the United States . . . The Communists are cheating the Arabs, making them believe they are on their side. But actually they are in league with the Zionists".

Can the Americans be so stupid? It is not simply a matter of stupidity. In the United States, with a few rare exceptions, it is money which decides which candidate, regardless of party, goes to Capitol Hill and it is money which decides who shall be president.

This explains America's weird policy of supporting the ludricous idea that Israel is a Western bastion" in the Middle East and that the powerless Arabs are the "bad guys" who "threaten world peace."

DOLLAR AID TO ISRAEL

Leftist newspapers which cry incessantly about censorship and the "mind control" they claim to find in Radio South Africa's news services and commentaries themselves implement a policy of selection and suppression indistinguishable from a thoroughgoing system of censorship. With this difference: it is far more efficient and it is never mentioned, so that few people know about it.

But accidents happen even in the best regulated establishments as when the *Times* of London on February 5, 1971, printed in its two early editions an article by David Nes, a man who spent 26 years in the United States Foreign Service and was Charge d'Affaires in Cairo immediately before and during the 1967 Middle East war.

The blunder was spotted in time to exclude this article from subsequent editions of the *Times*. Or did some watchful reader get hold of the first edition and raise the alarm?

And yet that article by David Nes contains little information of a kind not available to anyone who cares to search for it in the right places. After all, there is no real secret about United States aid to Israel. The information is all to be found in official documents in Washington, but it does not reach the public through the mass media; or the separate pieces of information are not brought together so as to reveal their real meaning.

The result is that statements of the kind made by an authoritative writer like Mr. Nes acquire the properties of dynamite and must be excluded from "respectable" organs of public instruction like the *Times* which pride themselves on their fearless policy of telling the truth, the whole truth and nothing but the truth.

The subject of the Nes article is America's special relationship with Israel, a subject which is of vital concern to all of us at a time when the Middle East trouble can be clearly seen as containing the essential elements of a third world war.

Here, then, are some of the documented facts which made an article written by an expert, too hot to handle.

In dollars and cents, America's assistance to Israel through the years, both governmental and private, has been prodigious. During the 20-year period 1948-68 the United States economic aid totalled $11,000m (eleven billion) while dollar transfers from private sources amounted to $25,000m (twenty-five billion), making a total of $36,000m or $1,400 per capita on a current Israeli population of 2,500,000. This greatly exceeds, on a per capita basis, United States assistance to any ally and compares to $35 per capita to the peoples of 13 neighbouring states (from most of which U.S. investors derive enormous revenues—*Editor*).

Since 1968 American assistance to Israel has greatly increased. Dollar transfers in 1970 reached $800m and in 1971 approached $1.5 billion.

David Nes describes as "unique also" Israel's almost total immunity from criticism in the United States, a situation hardly paralleled by any of America's European or Asian allies, many of whose faults and frailties are daily aired in American communications media. Why this immunity? Mr. Nes quotes the remark of the *New York Times* writer, James Reston, who said recently: ". . . you can put it down as a general rule that any criticism of Israel's policies will be attacked as anti-semitism".

James Reston is right. Merely to discuss these matters of obvious and most vital concern to all of us is to invite a charge of anti-semitism and a reaction of revulsion from ordinary people whose minds have been conditioned down the years by a never-ending campaign of psychological warfare.

Mr. Moshe Menuhin, father of Yehudi Menuhin, the world-famous violinist, is one of that courageous band of men of Jewish race and faith who are most unhappy about developments in the Middle East and have dared to say so.

They see in this vibrant Jewish nationalism called Zionism a force which could bring disaster to Jewish people everywhere and many of them, including writers like Alfred

Lilienthal, have suffered terrible persecutions for expressing this viewpoint.

This is as good an opportunity as any of stating our own basic position as a news analysing service. We believe in nationalism as an organic unifying, energy-releasing, courage-building force in history. Therefore, we cannot object to Jewish nationalism.

We believe, however, that people should all know the truth so that whatever policies they decide on, whether to pour more billions of dollars into Israel or to withhold aid, are based on the true facts and a correct interpretation of these facts.

Most people, we believe, would object most strongly (if they knew) to being drawn into the vortex of a nationalism which is not their own, harnessing their energies to alien interests and alien purposes.

The great challenge of our times is to dare to tear holes in the painted cloth of massively financed propaganda and psychological warfare and to get an occasional peep at what is really going on behind.

This is not so difficult once we have learned the trick of it. Even from the information supplied by the mass media it is often possible to detect the inconsistencies and contradictions and to find facts which could not be suppressed and which, correctly interpreted, tell us a story very different from the one we have been asked to believe.

Let us look at some of the facts which have emerged recently and see how much of the forbidden truth can be wrung out of them.

The establishment story, we need hardly remind our subscribers, is that in the strategically most important Middle East area we have a situation in which the Arabs are at war with the Israelis with the Soviet Union backing the Arabs and the United States backing the Israelis. Now read on:

• Sudan's Advocate-General, at the trial in August 1971 of the West German mercenary Rolf Steiner, accused Israel of having helped and encouraged secessionist rebels. The court was left in no doubt that the Government of Sudan has a massive dossier on Israeli involvement in recent efforts to overthrow the Nimeiry regime.

• The Sudanese rift with the Soviet Union was further widened, so we are told (and we can believe it) with the order by President Nimeiry's Government that Mr. Mikhail Orlov, the second senior Russian diplomat in Khartoum, and Mr. Stoyam Zaimov, the Bulgarian ambassador, must leave the country within 24 hours. This order came immediately after a quick counter-coup had overthrown the short-lived Communist regime. Simultaneously there was news of violent outcries in the Communist Press over President Nimeiry's severity in dealing with those who had tried to overthrow him.

Soviet backing for a coup which the Israelis were helping to promote was also plainly in evidence in Cairo where, immediately after the Communists had taken over and thrown Nimeiry in gaol, the Kremlin's ambassador urged the Egyptian Government to recognise the new regime without delay. President Sadat refused to comply—and it has since been made clear that both Egypt and Libya had a hand in helping to turn the tables against the Khartoum rebels.

Here, then, we have the Soviet Union and Israel apparently in the same camp (all highly secret, of course) in opposition to Arab control in the Sudan.

Is it any wonder that Communism's masters in the Kremlin found it necessary to send President Podgorny himself to Cairo with loud protestations of friendship to sign another "pact of friendship"? This was after similar efforts had been made to unseat President Sadat by similar rebels of the far-Left.

RUSSIA AND THE MIDDLE EAST

Surely this only confirms the accuracy of the following report, date-lined Haifa, June 8, 1970, which appeared in the *Chicago Tribune,* one of America's few major newspapers which have managed to preserve some measure of independence:

> David Ben-Gurion has told students here he believes the Soviet Union 'would not be anxious to help President Nasser in an all-out attempt to destroy Israel. Unfortunately, I cannot say that Nasser is not aiming at the total destruction of our state,' said the 83-year-old leader who recently resigned his seat in the Knesset, Israel's parliament.

'I am convinced the Soviet Union does not seek the destruction of Israel', he said. 'We must never forget that the Soviet Union strongly supported the formation of Israel and recognised the state as soon as I announced its creation on May 15, 1948. Russia supplied us with arms that helped us survive our war of independence. Present Soviet policy in the Middle East is a passing stage'.

Ben-Gurion said he could not accept popular current charges that the Soviet Union helped Israel at the beginning in hopes of using Israel as a stepping stone into the Middle East.

Since only a few individuals enjoy the privilege of knowing what motives are at work "behind the scenes" (to use Disraeli's expression) the leakage of a certain amount of embarrassing information is unavoidable, and such information is frequently published by mass media which do not understand what it really means.

Towards the end of July, 1971, news leaked out that Victor Louis (he's the Russian-Jewish journalist who sold the Svetlana Stalin and Krushchev biographies to the American *Time-Life* organisation) had been in Tel Aviv on "a delicate, quasi-official mission for Moscow." The words are quoted from the British leftist paper, *The Guardian*.

"These reports," said *The Guardian,*" "deepen the mystery surrounding the incipient Soviet-Israel contacts which have taken place in recent weeks."

The egregious Mr. Louis carried a Soviet passport. He travelled to Israel from Helsinki and afterwards left Tel Aviv for Bucharest, Rumania, being seen off at the airport by an Israel Foreign Ministry official. While in Tel Aviv, Mr. Louis stayed at the Samuel Hotel — but then his guest card at the hotel mysteriously disappeared!

Back in Moscow, Mr. Louis admitted that he had been in Tel Aviv — but only for a "medical check-up". Secret diplomacy was never called that before!

The return of Louis to Moscow via Bucharest reminds us of another item which was never brought to the attention of people in the West trying desperately to understand what was happening in the Middle East around the time of the Six-Day War.

Shortly before the Six-Day War, we now learn, the Rumanian Communist dictator Nicolas Ceausescu travelled to Moscow for a conference with the Kremlin "top brass". As soon as he returned to Bucharest, he announced that his government had decided to adopt a neutral position in the pending Middle East conflict.

Furthermore, reports the *Washington Observer,* Rumania and Israel entered into a trade pact, ensuring an abundance of Rumanian oil for the Israeli war machine. This was all that Defence Minister, Moshe Dayan, needed to unleash his tanks and airplanes in a devastating war against his country's neighbours.

How the pieces of a jig-saw puzzle fall into place once the player has correctly guessed what the picture is all about!

Time magazine reports that the Washington correspondent of Israel's most influential newspaper *Ha'aretz* "has suddenly become the luncheon companion most in demand among Soviet journalists".

Demonstrations by Jewish groups protesting at the treatment of Jews in the Soviet Union — exercises in protest which never had the ring of truth — faded out simultaneously all over Europe and the United States.

Add to all this the fact that when the Israeli Prime Minister, Mrs. Golda Meier (she is both an American and an Israeli citizen) attended the Socialist International Convention in Helsinki (at which the Soviet Bloc was powerfully represented) she quietly dropped several motions which were to have been introduced dealing with the subject of Jews in Russia.

Mystriously absent from Helsinki for a few days, Mrs. Meier was reported to have turned up at a remote village in Finnish Lapland, close to the Soviet Union's north-western frontier — for what purpose, if not to meet Soviet emissaries? And a month later Gideon Raphael, Director-General of the Israeli Foreign Office, while on a visit to Stockholm also performed a mysterious disappearing act, to be traced to the same remote village in Finnish Lapland. When the news leaked out Raphael's trip was described as "purely private," like Victor Louis's visit to Tel Aviv a month earlier.

It would be hard to exaggerate the importance of the fact that prominent liberal spokesmen are taking a new hard look at the Middle East situation and are "telling it as it is". Thus we find even inside the British Liberal Party and the British Labour Party elements who have dared to take up cudgels on behalf of an Arab population which has been dispossessed of its ancestral homeland. These liberal intellectuals, basically honest even if still grossly misguided on certain issues, are realising in increasing numbers the real nature of a Middle East conflict which, if allowed to escalate, could involve the whole world in the holocaust of a third world war.

A Western European intellectual honesty, the ultimate source of the so-called "might of the West," now shows signs of prevailing over the claims of political partisanship and of disrupting an old and well tried partnership.

Zionism on its own is powerless; it is powerful only to the extent that it can focus and control a host of other political forces, like the intellectual liberalism of the Western world.

THE JEWS IN RUSSIA

For what may be criticised here as Anti-Semitism is only the negative side of Zionism—G. K. Chesterton, The New Jerusalem.

How are we to understand and interpret the spate of newspaper reports about the persecution of Jews in the Soviet Union? And what bearing do all these reports have on the Middle East situation?

Questions like these are being asked since the recent trial in Leningrad of a group of people, including Jews, on a charge of attempting to hijack a Soviet airliner to Israel.

In many parts of the Western world there have been protest meetings, all arranged by local Jewish communities, at which complaints have been voiced about the treatment of Jews in the Soviet Union.

Reports of all these happenings have tended to add to the confusion in the public mind about the policies and actions of the Soviet Union and about the Middle East situation in particular.

Winston Churchill once described the Soviet Union as "a riddle, wrapped in a mystery, inside an enigma".

So far as Russia's internal affairs are concerned, we do not mind greatly if that country remains for ever a closed book. But when we find ourselves drawn into the orbit of a massive and elaborate process of mystification, then our ingenuity and powers of penetration are challenged, knowing as we do that our own safety depends on finding out what is happening and why.

We are mainly interest, of course, in what the Russians are doing outside Russia — in the Middle East for example, where an almost impenetrable fog of mental confusion has been generated in the last few years. We know that the confusion forms no part of Soviet action in the Middle East or anywhere else, but is only something which has been built into the reporting and propaganda which have accompanied the action.

We also know, or should know, that the situation of the Jews in Russia cannot be separated from the subject of what is happening in the Middle East. We feel we need to know more about the situation of the Jews in Russia if we are to understand what is happening today outside Russia.

We start off with a feeling that there is something implausible about some of these reports which have been circulating in the Western world about the persecution of Jews in Russia. The stories themselves, and the reactions to them, have not rung true.

We ask ourselves: How long has this been going on? If for a long time, then why the almost total silence on this subject all down the years? How, also, are we to explain the absence of a worldwide Jewish campaign of hostility against the Soviet Union and against Communism at a time when the Soviet Union appears to have joined forces with Egypt against Israel? What is being hidden behind all this smoke and smother?

Quite frankly, we do not believe that Russia's Jews are being persecuted. We believe that what is being represented to the world as persecution is little more than a quarrel or difference of opinion and attitude inside Russian Jewry on the subject of Zionism, or Jewish nationalism. A small, vehement minority wish to raise the banner of Zionism inside the Soviet Union, or they want to be allowed to go to Israel or the United States to throw themselves into the Zionist cause.

Many Jews in the Western world are afraid of what the Zionists are doing, but they are even more afraid of complaining aloud, because in the Western world Zionism is now all-powerful and triumphant.

Writes Alfred M. Lilienthal in his book *The Other Side of the Coin:*

"An even greater tragedy for us is that many people who have serious doubts about the course upon which Israel has embarked, and what the United States has partially underwritten, are too deeply frightened to say so. The writer never could present the massive record of pressures, suppression and terrorism employed against these frightened Americans, simply because the more submissive victims of Jewish nationalist pressure are usually too ashamed or too afraid to publicise their experiences."

There are now good reasons to believe that in the Soviet Union today it is the majority of the Jews who are afraid of Zionism — a complete reversal of the situation this side of the Iron Curtain. Russia's Jews who are today powerfully placed and highly influential, are afraid that a rabid Jewish nationalism could have a polarising effect on a latent anti-semitism in the Slav masses which has been suppressed since the Bolshevik Revolution but which has not been eradicated. Therefore, any manifestation of Zionist enthusiasm inside the Soviet Union must be harshly repressed.

For the rulers of Russia this is no new problem. After the revolution an element of Jewish nationalism was permitted to survive in the form of a socialist party called Poale Zion. But Poale Zion became an embarrassment to Jews who had helped to carry through the revolution and to millions of others who later poured into the Communist Party and the bureaucracy. Therefore, Poale Zion was suppressed or swallowed up by the monolithic Communist Party.

Interestingly enough, there was a Poale Zion Jewish socialist party in Britain until 1920 when it allowed itself to be swallowed up by the Labour Party for similar reasons.

Isaac Deutscher, an anti-Zionist, tells us: ". . . the most fanatical advocates of the suppression of Jewish parties were by no means the Russians — they were the Jews themselves, the Jewish Communists, the Yevsektsia (Jewish section of the Communist Party). I was in Russia at the time when these problems were hotly debated and I witnessed repeatedly how Russian Bolsheviks, among them Mikhail Kalinin, the President of the USSR, argued with the Jewish comrades trying to temper their fierce hostility towards the Zoinist idea, towards the remnants of the Bund (another Zionist group) and even towards Jewish clericalism. But the Jewish Communists felt that they had to be more orthodox, more 'kosher', more determined, than their Russian comrades."

What all this means is that Zionism has planted a split in the Jewish mind, since it is plainly impossible for the Jew to dissolve, as it were, into a non-Jewish population, prospering and exerting his maximum influence there, and at the same time exhibit himself to the world as a passionate advocate of a Jewish nationalism like Zionism.

For the Jewish people on both sides of the Iron Curtain, what makes the problem more difficult and dangerous is that nationalism, deep-rooted in human nature, once it has been experienced, has an almost irresistible appeal. Visitors to Israel tell us that Jews there, especially in the towns and cities, live in a perpetual seething ferment of nationalist enthusiasm. Nationalism produces an exciting release of the forces of the unconscious which, in the case of many Jews, had hitherto lain dormant and suppressed. On these nationalism works like a drug which, once tried, can never again be resisted.

The Jews in Russia who are getting into trouble are those who have been "hooked" by the Zionist psychology and are drawn to Israel, like moths to a flame, not hesitating even to hijack an airliner. Understandably, Zionist Jews in the rest of the world feel justified in interpreting the suppression of Zionism in the Soviet Union as persecution of the Jews.

There can be no doubt that the Jews have made an enormous, indeed a vastly disproportionate contribution to the creation of the Soviet Union. Deutscher tells us what is already well known, when he writes: "Jews played a very prominent part in the revolutionary movement." He also tells us that after the revolution the great majority of Russia's Jews with their urban tradition and their higher level of education, became white-collar workers and "entered en masse into the ranks of the post-revolutionary bureaucracy, into the party and state offices and institutions."

They also played a great part, he says in the universities where today, as teachers, they number some 25,000. All these people, who form a majority of Russian Jews, naturally do not want their position threatened by a small minority which has been caught up by Jewish nationalist enthusiasm, whose symbol, Israel, is outside Russia.

Even among non-Jews, the image and operations of Zionism is beginning to have a divisive and clarifying effect.

One example of this, small but highly significant, is the split which occurred recently in the British Labour Party between what are described as "pro-Arab and pro-Israel Members of Parliament." The issue is said to threaten the position of the party chairman, Mr. Ian Mikardo, who at a banquet on September 12 to celebrate the 50th anniversary of the affiliation of Poale Zion with the Labour Party, described a former Labourite Foreign Minister, Mr. Ernest Bevin, as an "anti-semite" and accused Foreign Office diplomats of being "pro-Arab".

Since the above was written, a report from one Dev Murarka, has been published in the South African morning Press, from which the following is a brief extract: ". . . there is no sign of any persecution of the Jews as a community. They go about their daily business and are a prominent part of the professional intelligentsia which occupies a conspicuous position in Soviet society."

Needless to say, it suits the Soviet Union admirably to be accused of persecuting the Jews at a time when many Arabs are beginning to "smell a rat" in this Middle East "alliance" of Russia and the Arab States against Israel.

"The Jewish racial myth flows from the fact that the words *Hebrew, Israelite, Jew, Judaism,* and the *Jewish people* have been used synonymously to suggest a historic continuity. But this is a misuse. These words refer to different groups of people with varying ways of life in different periods in history."—Alfred M. Lilienthal, *What Price Israel?*

ENCOURAGING SIGNS

Recently, the arch-liberal Malcolm Muggeridge has admitted that modern Liberalism has been a ghastly failure.

What is happening is that liberalism is being poisoned by its own effluents. People simply cannot continue to hold a set of beliefs which produce a never-ending succession of appalling results.

We see the disillusionment of these liberals as one of the encouraging signs that liberal intellectualism is a receding historical wave. The only reason why this recession on the intellectual front is not more plainly noticeable is that it has not been accompanied by any weakening on the part of those giant moneyed forces which have always patronised and employed this intellect — on the contrary, while the intellectual side of the partnership grows weaker, the moneyed half grows stronger.

Meanwhile, we may draw some encouragement from the knowledge that the moneyed forces depend completely on the partnership with a rootless intellect which it can use as its executive instrument and, perhaps most important of all, to conduct the battle on the propaganda front to mask the real motives at work.

The situation of the world conspiracy can thus be compared with that of an airman who, while still moving at high speed towards his destination, begins to fear that an obvious leak in his fuel tank may prevent him from ever getting there.

As the mark of permissible evil envelopes us more and more there is awakened in the soul of Western man a compulsive passion for the truth. The stage is reached when dispelling the murk becomes more exciting, more satisfying than any of the economic and purely personal rewards of compliance.

How brightly the flame of life burns within us depends on how much or how little real freedom we are able to gain for ourselves. And all freedom begins in the mind. Every time we dismantle or dissolve some falsehood which has shackled our minds, there follows a liberation and release of our vital forces.

Rise and begin this very moment, and say: *Now is the time to be up and doing; now is the time to fight!*—Thomas a' Kempis, The Imitation of Christ.

A SHORT LIST OF BOOKS FOR FURTHER READING:

None Dare Call it Conspiracy, Gary Allen

The Captive Nations, Bernadine Bailey

The Opinion Makers, Ivor Benson

A Message from Southern Africa, Ivor Benson

The Red Pattern of World Conquest, Eric Butler

The New Unhappy Lords, A. K. Chesterton

Who Shall Inherit the Earth?, A. T. Culwick

Ethnological Elements of Africa, R. Gayre of Gayre

The Middle East Crisis, Sir John Glubb

The Struggle for World Power, George Knupffer

What Price Israel?, Alfred M. Lilienthal

Far and Wide, Douglas Reed

The Dispossessed Majority, Wilmot Robertson

The Naked Capitalist, W. Cleon Skousen

None Dare Call It Treason, John A. Stormer

Imperium, Francis Parker Yockey

THE CANADIAN LEAGUE OF RIGHTS
BOX 2797
VANCOUVER 3, B. C.

<u>**SUPPORT THE AUSTRALIAN LEAGUE OF RIGHTS**</u>

The League of Rights is a non-party political organization.

Its objectives may be summarised as follows:

* Loyalty to God and the Crown.

* Fostering the strengthening of ties between the member nations of the British Crown Commonwealth.

* Support of private ownership of property and genuine competitive enterprises.

* Defence of the Rule of Law.

* Opposition to all policies of totalitarianism, irrespective of their label.

The League is not motivated exclusively by opposition to Communism, and to other threats to individual freedom and dignity; it constantly holds up the vision of a world that could be: one of expanding freedom and security for all, in which every individual can participate freely in association with his fellows to build the finest Civilization yet created by man.

The League is a new type of organization, offering an opportunity for service to those who want to do something purposeful with their lives, in opposition to those who seek to drive man down the scale of existence and to deny him his divine destiny.

VICTORIA: Box 1052J, Melbourne 3001,
273 Little Collins Street, Melbourne

NEW SOUTH WALES: Box 2957 Sydney 2001

QUEENSLAND: Box 17, Alderley 4051

SOUTH AUSTRALIA: Box 1297L Adelaide 5001

WESTERN AUSTRALIA: Box 16, Inglewood 6052

Recommended Publications

AUSTRALIA: *Intelligence Survey,* published monthly, provides a vital intelligence system for the responsible individual who desires to know what is really going on in the world. Specimen copies available on request. By private subscription only. $5.00 per annum, post free.

On Target, published weekly, is a news-commentary which keeps the busy person abreast of the most significant developments in the cold war. By private subscription only. $4 per annum, post free.

Ladies' Line. The steady expansion in the circulation of this publication demonstrates that it is providing a real service for thinking Australian women concerned about the attacks on the undergirding values of their society. Published fortnightly by Queensland Council of the Australian League of Rights, P.O. Box 17, Alderley, Brisbane, 4051. Subscription Rate: $3.00 per annum.

BRITAIN: *On Target,* published by The British League of Rights. Subscription $4.00 per annum. Enquiries to, 65 Craddocks Avenue, Ashtead, Surrey, England.

CANADA: *On Target* and *Canadian Intelligence Service* published by The Canadian League of Rights at $7.00 and $5.00 respectively. Enquiries to, Canadian League of Rights, Flesherton, Ontario.